THE KINGDOM QUEST

Preparing to Church Plant in the
Post-Christian West

Tom Johnston
Mike Chong Perkinson

PraxisMedia

Copyright © 2019 The Praxis Center for Church Development

2nd edition published 2023.
All rights reserved.

No part of this book may be reproduced, or stored in a retrieval system, or transmitted in any form or by any means, electronic, mechanical, photocopying, recording, or otherwise, without express written permission of the publisher.

ISBN-13: 9780982272732

Cover design by: Jodie McCay
Library of Congress Registration Number: TXu1-338-683
Printed in the United States of America

Dedication

To all the church planters, especially all those willing to roll the dice with Jesus more than once. You are our heroes. May the Lord bless you, your family and your mission.

CONTENTS

Title Page
Copyright
Dedication
Forward
Acknowledgements
Chapter 1 - So, you want to plant a church?   1
Part 1 - DNA Formation   22
Chapter 2 - Who Are You?   23
Chapter 3 - What Do You Have to Say?   36
Chapter 4 - Are you Ready?   45
Chapter 5 - What is Your Quest?   58
Part 2 – DNA Transmission & Multiplication   65
Chapter 6 - Who is Your Community?   66
Chapter 7 - Where are You Called?   82
Chapter 8 - How Will You Form This New Community?   91
Chapter 9 - Who Will Walk Alongside You?   105
Chapter 10 - How Will You Complete Your Training?   115
Appendix – Determining Your Personal Values   121

FORWARD

Wow, it's a privilege to write a *forward* for a book such as this. Tom Johnston and Mike Perkinson are both good friends of mine—and they are a couple of my heroes.

These guys are a generation younger than me and represent the continuum of fruitfulness that accompanies those who are forced to plant churches as the best way of making disciples. They took the ball when it was handed off and are moving it down the field with precision.

This book will challenge you from your hair to your toenails. These guys will mess with your head in every chapter from their challenge, "You cannot reproduce what you do not incarnate," to the illuminating story of a young man realizing that he had to die to being cool if he wants to plant a church that will communicate with a post-Christian world.

Tom and Mike are veteran planters, pastors and multipliers. Making disciples is their heritage and their nature. They fully understand the need of a doctor to spend time with the sick. Their comments about keeping our hearts pure while intentionally invading a dirty stable are the currency of disciple-makers.

Perhaps the best part of the book is the understanding that we must "be" before we "do." Psalm 1 illustrates godly man. It says whatever he does will prosper. But, it first describes healthy inputs to his being. The problem is that whatever we do usually prospers. These authors are asking you to do right things because you *became* the right person. Incarnate so you can reproduce.

Read on,

Ralph Moore
Author, *Starting a New Church*

ACKNOWLEDGEMENTS

Special thanks to our proof readers *Rev. Catherine Maillet, Jodie McCay, Donna Fry and Dr. Eugene Luke.* We are grateful to God for your efforts to make our writing intelligent and comprehensible. There is no more difficult job on earth.

CLARIFYING COMMENTS

With the proliferation of books, models, and processes that have developed over the past 25 years, we thought it might be helpful to tip our hand here and share with you the driving presuppositions of our thinking. There will be many things stated in this book that will easy to understand, some that could be misunderstood, and others that could be missed all together. We want to insure that understanding and effective communication truly takes place from our hearts to your heart and ultimately, from God's heart to yours for the glory and expansion of His Kingdom by those who faithfully declare their love for Him and His people through this process called church planting.

Communication is an amazing process. We are amazed that communication actually takes place. That is, the receptor of the communiqué actually hears the words and heart of the sender, not only understanding the literal word(s) but grasping the heart or spirit of the words as well. Yet only does a potential for misunderstanding exist, we recognize that it is intensified when we have only words on a page to express our intended meaning. A plethora of pitfalls must be avoided in writing: a poor choice of words; words too direct or too bold without proper or appropriate context; words that are not direct enough; personal biases filtering words, interpreting potential meanings that are not being said; and personal biases and issues of the author(s) and reader that could cloud the process. Even with all those risks, somehow people still write and are understood. May understanding from us to you take place and more so from God to you transpire as you endeavor on this Kingdom Quest.

The reason we want to "tip our hand" is that we have discovered that there are points where people have misinterpreted our statements. Our assumption can only be that we did not communicate them as effectively as we had hoped. Our desire is then to state up front some of the issues that we sense could be misunderstood as you journey with us in this book. Let us now list for you some of our fundamental presuppositions.

We believe in the Church, the Bride of Christ, and celebrate the Church. However we are not all that pleased with how we have dressed up the Bride of Christ at times, adding or taking away from her beauty and weighing her down in ways that have made the Church rather weak and ineffective, rather than being full of God's power and transforming love.

We believe the process of "doing" church, particularly in the Western world, has been more focused on developing people who attend church rather than developing disciples who are the Church, living as a kingdom of priests and incarnating Christ in their homes, at their jobs, and in every life situation radiating God's love, forgiveness, mercy, and grace as followers of Christ. This is not to say that every pastor is primarily interested in developing church attendees. Many desire and contend for more, but the form or wineskin we employ largely facilitates the development of church attendees. We do a great job training people to learn the Christian lingo, our specific and particular slant or brand of Christianity (e.g. the Pentecostal brand, the Bible-based brand, the Post-Modern brand, the Social Activist brand, the Non-Denominational or Generic brand, etc.), how to act and worship in the corporate gathering learning to do what is appropriate and acceptable for our theological persuasion – essentially how to do church for two hours a week. What is missing in many circles is how to be an actual follower of Christ, how to live as a son/daughter of God the rest of the week, how to be a part of a community of believers who care for each other while they impact the neighborhood around them.

We believe that teaching includes the pulpit, classroom, and training venues, but should not be limited to or solely based upon such procedures. Teaching is best transmitted life to life ("more is caught than taught") as the young apprentice seeks to learn from the Rabbi not only what the Rabbi knows, but also what he does, and more importantly, longs to become like the Rabbi. In the same vein, the Jedi Master, Yoda passed on his wisdom to the young Jedi in training, Luke Skywalker, helping him tap into the force within. The desire of Luke was to not only know what Yoda knew, to do what Yoda did, but to be like Yoda – a Jedi. May each of us find the true force within, the power of the living God in the person of the Holy Spirit.

We believe the New Testament neither mentions nor

validates any form or model of doing church. Rather the New Testament simply tells us that whatever form of wineskin we employ it must contain the pure wine of the Gospel of the Kingdom. This is not to say the wineskin is not important but to make quite plain that what is significant is not the wineskin or form, no matter how cool it is. It is the wine that calms the thirst of the human soul and we must learn to become good winemakers. The ingredients to mix the wine are provided in Matthew 22:37-39 (the Great Commandments); Matthew 20:18-20 (the Great Commission); and Acts 2:42 (the Great Community). The wineskin one creates should be based on one's calling, gifting, and cultural context and, of course, made with excellence.

We believe the entrepreneurial launch model and the strategic plan approach that has been implemented in our church planting process have been beneficial and helpful for the establishment of many churches, and for that, we are grateful. However, our concern is that when you adopt an entrepreneurial launch model or incorporate a strategic plan without thinking through one's ecclesiology or philosophy of ministry, then it presumes a model. You will tend to assume the launching of a public service ("going public") as your pathway, tend to staff to the mission (product creation and sales) rather than loving God, loving others, and making disciples (developing people) as the mission, and tend to be consumer driven, seek to attract people to a service rather than be a blessing and service to the community, spending most of your time, energy and money on the big weekend service.

We believe the issue of church growth is not about the size of a church. That is, big is not better, nor is small better. Dan Hawkins, the head coach of the football program at University of Colorado says, "Big is not better. Better is better." There are plenty of large and small churches that are healthy and vibrant and plenty that are not. At the end of Jesus' ministry he had a small church, if you will, of only 120. They were not your average 120 people. They were radically and totally committed to the Gospel and gave their lives to it and changed the course of human history as a result. On a negative note, 18 men following an evil leader changed the face of our current situation as they boarded planes on September 11, 2001. There are countless examples in history of smaller and larger numbers of dedicated individuals impacting society, culture, and even history. The issue is not whether or not we are growing in size, we pray that we do, but that we are growing in the making of disciples – better is better – whether big or small. Mike's pastor, the late Roy Hicks, Jr. once said, "Just because you have a lot of people it does not mean you have a church. It only means you have a lot of people." Remember what we have already said:, the New Testament neither validates nor invalidates the mega-church or the house church models. It simply tells us to love God, love others as we love ourselves, and to make disciples as we live our lives. The content of the Christian "wine" (Christian life in community) is found in Acts 2:42-47. The language of the early church is built around the word "devotion," as they were devoted to the apostle's teaching, the fellowship, the breaking of bread, and the prayers. This is our heart as we seek to help you through this book on your quest.

INTRODUCTION

And Jesus came and said to them, "All authority in heaven and on earth has been given to me. Go therefore and make disciples of all nations, baptizing them in the name of the Father and of the Son and of the Holy Spirit, teaching them to observe all that I have commanded you. And behold, I am with you always, to the end of the age" (Matthew 28:18-20 ESV).

    It might startle some in the church multiplication world to know that Jesus never gave us a command to plant churches. For that matter, we are not convinced that Jesus came to start a new religion either. It would seem He came to establish two great relationships: loving God with everything we have, and loving our neighbor as ourselves. Based on the two great relationships (Great Commandments as they have been called), we find the Great Commission: Jesus sent us to make disciples, instructing us to teach them, our disciples, what was commanded ("A new commandment I give to you, that you love one another: just as I have loved you, you also are to love one another." John 13:34 ESV) and to show them how to observe, or to do what was commanded. This was the life and mission of those original followers of Christ - to go everywhere and do everything they could to make disciples of every kind of people on the face of the Earth. Not once did he mention "planting churches." In fact, the only time he talks about the church is when he defines it as "people" and says that He will build it (Matthew 16:18).

    One might argue here that church planting is the greatest way to make disciples. We do not argue that it does help or could help in making disciples. In our experience it inevitably leads more to making church attendees than disciples of Christ. We suggest that making disciples is a great way of planting a church, developing leaders, and fostering a movement that might impact our cities, and dare we say, our world.

Jesus seems more concerned with the organic reality of the Church, its DNA or genetic code, than with the structural or procedural concerns that overwhelm us in the 21st century. We are not saying the structural or procedural issues are not important. They are, but that was not the primary focus of our Master and should not be ours either. In other words, Jesus was more focused on the building and development of people into disciples than the establishment of an institution. In the New Testament there is a noted lack of instruction on how to employ cool outreach methods (although miracles are a great marketing tool for attracting crowds) and absolutely nothing about launching a public worship service. The book of Acts does make it quite evident that the Church started at a point in time, and it could be construed as something like a launch. It might be better said that what is recorded in scripture is the birth of the Church, not its launch. Organizations and businesses are launched. Organic, living entities like the Church are birthed – you give birth to babies. That the infant Church was born at Pentecost is rather remarkable and the Pauline churches that were birthed had a point in time they started. We do not argue against a "launch" per se, but assert the New Testament does not place its emphasis on the planting of churches. Rather it stresses the corporate reality of a "lived" faith where people seek to make disciples as a part of their lives taking the command to make disciples personally as well as a command from Jesus for the Church corporately. More accurately, the instruction to the Church corporate was a missional injunction founded on a way of life. With that said, we see there is strong instruction in the pages of the New Testament and in the life of the Messiah for following Him, so that the disciples could learn what He knew, do what He did, and eventually become like Him. He did not teach the methodologies, techniques and skills for the young and eager apprentices that often comprise the foundation of our training in the 21st century Church. Rather, He embodied and lived out the way, through how He conducted His life and ministry. He *showed* them the way, *showed* them the truth, and *showed* them the life. As we look at Jesus' life and ministry, it appears He wasn't as concerned about the things that so often concern us when it comes to church planting: money, marketing, hip services, cool people, etc. Such concerns just didn't seem to register on Jesus' radar as significant.

If you'll permit us to engage in some foolishness here (or maybe you think we have already engaged in foolishness), we'd like to take a modern look at Jesus sending of the twelve early on in His ministry. We'll cite the text as it is then modernize it for you. That is how it might sound today if Jesus were here. Here is the text as it is from the New Living Translation.

> *Jesus sent the twelve disciples out with these instructions: "Don't go to the Gentiles or the Samaritans, but only to the people of Israel—God's lost sheep. Go and announce to them that the Kingdom of Heaven is near. Heal the sick, raise the dead, cure those with leprosy, and cast out demons. Give as freely as you have received! "Don't take any money with you. Don't carry a traveler's bag with an extra coat and sandals or even a walking stick. Don't hesitate to accept hospitality, because those who work deserve to be fed. Whenever you enter a city or village, search for a worthy man and stay in his home until you leave for the next town. When you are invited into someone's home, give it your blessing. If it turns out to be a worthy home, let your blessing stand; if it is not, take back the blessing. If a village doesn't welcome you or listen to you, shake off the dust of that place from your feet as you leave. I assure you, the wicked cities of Sodom and Gomorrah will be better off on the judgment day than that place will be. "Look, I am sending you out as sheep among wolves. Be as wary as snakes and harmless as doves. But beware! For you will be handed over to the courts and beaten in the synagogues. And you must stand trial before governors and kings because you are my followers. This will be your opportunity to tell them about me—yes, to witness to the world. When you are arrested, don't worry about what to say in your defense, because you will be given the right words at the right time. For it won't be you doing*

> the talking—it will be the Spirit of your Father speaking through you." (Matthew 10:5-20)

Now, we'll take the text and allow Jesus to instruct a group of young church planters who are ready to embark upon their dream of planting a church in the 21st century. Imagine that they have just worked through *Beyond Church Planting*, completed *The Quest* church planting intensive, followed their pastor or leader around for the past 12 months watching everything He did, and then find themselves released with full authority after the intensive to now go and plant a church. The Messiah, in a moment of sober instruction, gives a few last minute morsels of wisdom to the eager planters as He sends the church planters out with these instructions. Here is our illustrative paraphrase:

> *Be sure you go to the right people that my Father has called you to. You are not called to everyone, but to a specific someone, a people, a group. Try not to do everything and be everything, but simply be the son/daughter that my Father has created you to be, and through your God given identity as a son/daughter and with His grace empowerment you will do mighty exploits for my Father. Of course market studies and demographics are helpful, but knowing yourself and more importantly knowing My Father are preeminent. Now go and announce to them that the Kingdom of Heaven is near – that there is Great News of hope and life for all and it has come to them this day.*

> *Here is how you will do this. When you reach out to the felt needs of people you will heal the sick, curing those with AIDS and cancers, raise the dead, and cast out demons. I realize that you cannot do this without the power of the Holy Spirit, but be without fear for I am with you. As you have been living these things with Me already, this way of life is not new to you. Simply go and be the person you have already been. And don't forget to give as freely as you have received!*

As you go out to plant your church, don't worry about money or writing a church plant proposal requesting funding. Just go; and for that matter don't take any money with you. I'll take care of your needs. Remember I will provide and build my Church. You won't have to do that, just obey what I have told you to live out as my son/daughter and it will happen. Remember to connect people to their Father in Heaven, not so much to the church plant. It is only a vehicle by which My presence is incarnated through a community where people can find the two relationships that matter most, loving God and loving others as themselves, and then to share that love by making disciples.

When you come to the town or city which I am sending you to, be sure to search for the man or woman of peace who will allow you access into a network of relationships where the Kingdom of Heaven can be shared. I've already prepared that persons' heart to receive you. Begin your church plant relationally, and keep it relational as you grow, because life is about the two great relationships. If it so happens that you are not able to find the man or woman of peace, and the people do not welcome you or listen to you, then graciously move on from those relationships and seek out people who are receptive to the Good News of the Kingdom. Don't make people receive me or anger them because they don't want to. I'll send someone else to reach them. Go on and love those who are ready to receive Me.

You need to know that this endeavor of church planting is difficult and full of twists and turns that could dislodge your faith. As a matter of fact, I am sending you out as sheep among wolves. It would be good if you were as wise as snakes and harmless as doves. But I should warn you that there will be many times that you will encounter people who are not for Me and are even antagonistic to the Gospel. But don't be afraid, for this will be your opportunity to tell them about me, to witness to the city, officials, and key corporate executives. When things go bad, and they will, don't worry about what to say in your defense. Your reputation or success is not what is significant here but how you will live in My Name as a humble man/woman of faith, who has come to bring the Good News of hope, not to judge who is in or out. At just the right time you will be given the right words to say. Always remember, it won't be you doing the talking. It will be the Spirit of your Father speaking through you. Be wise, be prepared, and always trust My Father, for when you do He will do things that will humble you and blow your mind.

Let Me summarize what I have said to you before you go. Go to the people God has called you to and made you for; be yourself and function within your grace empowerment; trust my Spirit to advertise for you through signs, wonders and transformed lives. Don't worry about money, but live out all that I have commanded you. Find the man or woman of peace who will lead you into a network of relationships. Trust Me for the words when called upon to proclaim the Good News of the Kingdom. Oh and did I mention, it will cost you everything.

What Jesus really cared about was *people* not a system that could simply multiply His influence, or a slick slogan or edgy philosophy that could produce a quick surge in public awareness. For Jesus, ministry was not a profession but rather a calling that flowed from a relationship with the Father. It was a way of life which involved connecting people with their heavenly Father, not just getting them into the Temple. In many cases, the Temple was the last place people could connect with the Father. In Jesus' day is was a place where if they did find the Father they would quickly lose the joy of their relationship with Him, as the religious leaders weighed them down with their own interpretations and required activities in what it meant to be a true follower of God. The goal of Jesus for each person was rather simple, and it was to have people follow Him as "the Way, the Truth and the Life" (John 14:6), to be His disciple, and in doing so would come to know God the Father. Thereby, they would become a community of disciples engaged in transforming their culture and world. Jesus was not looking for attendees, or believers. He was, and is, looking for *disciples* – those who want to know what He knows, do what He does, and be like Him. That is precisely how He sent His original band of brothers from Mt. Olive with a commission, a Great Commission: **make more disciples**.

It should be noted that Jesus' ministry did attract people by the thousands, but we must be clear to state here that He was not focused on attracting people as much as He was on incarnating the truth (John 1:14; Romans 15:18) and showing the world the Father.

Here we are 20 Centuries later, seeking to be obedient to Christ, seeking to make more disciples in a world that is increasingly more spiritually hungry, aware and open. *To that end disciple-making must be the focus of all our church planting efforts.* Not just as an *outcome* of church planting, but rather as the *means* of church planting.

A great deal of church planting methodology used in the Western world is a combination of accessing consumer-felt needs and marketing spiritual products for people to vend. This is then a huge roadblock to the disciple-making focus, as the goal is attendance, not discipleship. It is hoped that discipleship is the final byproduct, but this is rarely the case. The Conversion growth rate of the church in America continues to hover around 5%, with 95% of the growth coming from transfer.

It has been said that the church, in a large part, has been reduced to being a vendor of spiritual goods and services. Whichever church has the best product and environment is the one who wins the loyal support of its constituency. The pressure on the church is then to satisfy its customer base and continue to be a vendor of spiritual goods and services, setting us up to be in competition with each other for the local Christian market share of our city. But is this really what the church is supposed to do? Nothing is wrong with trying to meet people where they are or ministering to felt needs. We are not challenging those activities, but we question the whole concept of ***doing*** church. In contrast, the New Testament seems to lay a foundation that tells us the Church is a community of believers who live out the message of the Cross. What we don't find in the New Testament is the early Christians trying to ***do*** church. Rather, what we do find is a community of disciples who are the church. It seems that we spend so much of our time and energy trying to ***do*** church that we forget to actually ***be*** the church. Perhaps that is largely why the church seems so impotent in its ability to reach our world, and why so many church plants either don't live or grow. Simply winning over another church's members as a customer base simply changes the brand names, rather than better meeting their spiritual needs. We market our message well to those who are already in the faith, but not to those who are outside the fold. How does this help us in making disciples?

Scripture makes it plain that Jesus came "to seek and save what was lost" (Luke 19:10 NIV). That is precisely what drives the heart of the Church. We are called to be a community of believers who not only embrace each other well, but also reach out to the world in an understandable language and style. In this we might live out for them the greatest message on the planet. It's not as important how we do church as it is that we are the church. This generation is crying out for something real and tangible that can explain the greater mysteries of our existence. We believe people know there is something more, they just don't know where to find it and all too often find themselves leaving church services hungry for something more.

In simple language, unless we provide a relational environment though which people can encounter God, as we are encountering Him, then we have done nothing more than creative marketing that has forgotten to provide a quality product. The Church is then analogous to a family that provides a wonderful meal for their neighborhood. They invite everyone to come for dinner. As people walk in they smell the delightful aroma of a home cooked meal, enjoy the ambiance provided by the followers, the music and the warm greeting by the members of the family. The embrace is so loving and the feeling of belonging and acceptance is near perfect. The anticipation grows for the meal, light snacks are provided to help curb the appetite and build towards the main course. To the surprise of the guests no meal is served. Rather it is described in great detail with PowerPoint presentations and even a movie clip that enriches the picture of the meal for the hearers. The guests leave the house with a great idea of what the meal is but still find themselves hungry. Although the service and hospitality at the house were great, near perfect, it did not meet the great need of hunger within; and so, the guests go elsewhere in search of food to satisfy their hunger. In our modern day churches we often have the relational dynamics down, the ambiance, mood altering worship, technology, the relevant sermons, etc., but we forget to provide the actual meal -- the stuff that actually makes us the Church. The atmosphere where a real life God-encounter can take place and people can feast on the Lord to satisfy the deeper spiritual hunger of their souls. People don't go to a sports bar to watch soap operas. Since we are the Church, maybe we should not hold back on what we do. So that people will encounter God as He is. It's one thing for people to come to our churches and leave hungry because we do not provide a meal. It is entirely another for people to come to our churches and experience the meal and find themselves with a choice to eat or not. At least if they leave hungry, they do so because they chose to reject the Lord." (Johnston & Perkinson, *New Testament Trilogy: Our God, Ourselves, Our Community*, p. 69, edited)

Jesus told His disciples as He tells us today: **"But you will receive power when the Holy Spirit comes on you; and you will be my witnesses in Jerusalem, and in all Judea and Samaria, and to the ends of the earth."** (Acts 1:8) The assignment is simple and the power to accomplish it has been given. This is not a power that we can utilize for our simple enjoyment. God help us not reduce the power of the Holy Spirit to some personal experience of goose bumps that makes us tingle all over or some moment of ecstasy in the Spirit. As wonderful as this might be, it is only a small part of what the power of the Holy Spirit is about. Jesus gave the Holy Spirit to the Church so that we might fulfill the assignment given. God saved us because He loves us and He empowers us because He wants to touch the world through us. The abundant life can only be had when we give away the life that Jesus so freely gave us. Let's move forward, with the power of the Holy Spirit in us, and be the witnesses Jesus instructed us to be. The world needs to see Jesus in us. We are the Bible they are reading. **"But we have this treasure in jars of clay to show that this all-surpassing power is from God and not from us."** (2 Corinthians 4:7)

Unfortunately, our entrepreneurial, business model-driven

approach to church planting feeds on the consumerism in the society, and fuels a weakening of the Church in the West, as we get people "churched" (since they were "unchurched") as opposed to calling them to committed discipleship in Christ where they live the "way" of Christ. This book seeks to challenge and change that approach.

In this book, you will not find the latest tips, techniques and tricks to make your church really cool and attract some marginal Christian religionists or the disgruntled from the church down the street (95% of church growth in America is still transfer growth, with only 5% coming from conversion). What this book will focus on is people - the people involved in making disciples and those they seek to reach for Christ.

Don't misunderstand. The authors are all about starting new Christian church communities. We want to see those become disciple-making communities, multiplying disciples and themselves, seeing more and better disciples emerging all over the place. Our desire is to see disciple making communities that have an impact on their neighborhoods, towns, cities, regions, and world. So, what does reading this book do for you? We hope to give you some core biblical principles from the New Testament to organize your thinking about church and church planting, and give you some simple, practical steps from the ministry of Jesus as you seek to implement this new ministry endeavor. We want to see you become effective in making disciples of Jesus, and in doing so, give birth to a church that flows from your life and relationship with God.

If you hear a slight edge in our voice, it is because the status quo in our modern day church and in our church planting processes (not all mind you) is not only costing us the battle, but is also costing us the spiritual war in the West. George Barna's work, *The Revolution,* makes it quite clear that thousands if not millions are disgruntled with church, some for the wrong reasons, but many for the right reasons. In a Barna Update entitled "A Faith Revolution Is Redefining "Church," (October 10, 2005) written by the Barna Research Group we find some revealing prognostications.

One of the most eye-opening portions of the research contained in the book describes what the faith community may look like twenty years from now. Using survey data and other cultural indicators he has been measuring for more than two decades, Barna estimates that the local church is presently the primary form of faith experience and expression for about two-thirds of the nation's adults. He projects that by 2025 the local church will lose roughly half of its current "market share" and that alternative forms of faith experience and expression will pick up the slack. Importantly, Barna's studies do not suggest that most people will drop out of a local church to simply ignore spirituality or be freed up from the demands of church life. Although there will be millions of people who abandon the entire faith community for the usual reasons – hurtful experiences in churches, lack of interest in spiritual matters, prioritizing other dimensions of their life – a growing percentage of church dropouts will be those who leave a local church in order to intentionally increase their focus on faith and to relate to God through different means.

That growth is fueling alternative forms of organized spirituality, as well as individualized faith experience and expression. Examples of these new approaches include involvement in a house church, participation in marketplace ministries, and use of the Internet to satisfy various faith-related needs or interests, and the development of unique and intense connections with other people who are deeply committed to their pursuit of God.

We cannot continue to *do* church, and by association, church planting that reproduces that sterile form of a consumer-driven church as we have done in the past. We, along with countless others are passionate about the West experiencing what the global Christian community enjoys - revival and unprecedented growth and influence. Christianity continues to grow and prosper in all parts of the world EXCEPT North America and Western Europe. It's not too late. We must return to the business of making true, biblical disciples of Jesus Christ, and the best way to do that is starting new disciple making communities called "churches."

As you read on remember this: this adventure you are about to embark on is epic in proportion. It is no less than a quest to see the Kingdom of God extended into the lives of men, women and children. As you read, remember it is not about you. It is about Jesus and those He is calling to Himself. Keep your focus on Him, so that you can truly have eyes for the harvest.

May the Lord provoke you to love and good deeds as you read this book!

Tom Johnston & Mike Chong Perkinson

CHAPTER 1 - SO, YOU WANT TO PLANT A CHURCH?

    We were training some 150 or so denominational leaders and church planters in a conference in Boston when Mike asked a young church planter during the break for his reflections of the first session and was pleasantly surprised by his rather honest answer as he replied, "I'm really convicted by what you are saying. I came here to learn how to plant a cool, postmodern church and just realized that God has not called me to be cool." As the day went on, this young church planter came to realize that what he was venturing out to do had less to do with Jesus than it did with him, the packaging, the wineskin, the form. There was very little thought about the substance of the Church. As the seminar came to an end, he came up to Tom and with great humility asked for prayer.

    We are excited that you are on this venture of planting a church. God help us find more people in our day and age that will risk what you are risking for the purpose of His Kingdom advancement. Like the young man in our seminar, we often encounter people who plant churches myriad reasons. They often have less to do with Jesus and the lost and more to do with starting an organization and franchising it, with being cool, with building the "anti" church because of our most recent church catastrophe or disagreement, etc. We acknowledge that the God we all know uses frail human vessels to carry out His will and incarnate His presence in an ever needy and tired world. We are not sure that one can ever have completely pure motivations this side of heaven without some sense of the flesh contending for the spotlight, notoriety. All of us often want to prove something about ourselves, our theology, and/or our philosophy of ministry and style, or even getting even. Our point here is that we haven't met many church planters who are driven by love to plant their churches, or because of a heart that is absolutely broken for the people they are called to love and to bring the Good News of the Kingdom. Church planters who find themselves weeping over their cities, like Jesus wept over Jerusalem, broken for their cities, longing to find ways to incarnate the presence of the One who brings salvation, life, healing, and restoration of people, and to also restore what it means to really be human and live together as a community and family on this planet called Earth.

The Continuum of Community: Both/And

This Kingdom quest of church planting you are embarking upon involves a great deal of processing, potentially a dismantling or realignment, at least in part, of our theological understanding of God and the Church. Let us take a moment to deal with the reality of our understanding of inclusion, the "both/and" when it comes to the church.

It is important for you to know what kind of church you are going to plant and how it fits in within the Biblical parameters and the historic framework of the Church over the past 20 centuries. What we are referring to here is not what one can or cannot do as the church but what is it that makes us the Church. You know the fundamentals, the foundational realities common to all churches that follow Christ regardless of denominational or theological persuasion. We are glad that you want to plant a church but would like you to consider this question: **"What kind of church am I going to plant?"**

In our modern world we do not pause to consider the ontological realities of the Church as much as we focus on the pragmatic and missional components. Using the "wine" and "wineskin" imagery from scripture, our Churches in the West tend to focus almost exclusively on the "wineskin", the form or model of church without giving much thought to the "wine" – the stuff of life that actually is contained in the wineskin. It is not that churches ignore the "wine." All too often we simply assume its quality and then spend our time and energy on the container instead.

One can have an excellent container or bottle for the "wine" but if it is weak or diluted then no matter how beautiful the container people will not seek out the "wine." They will look for another "wine" that might satisfy the thirst within. Making an excellent container or wine bottle based on the market you are attempting to reach is good ("both/and") but it might be better for us to consider the "wine" first to make sure it is genuine and full of life. Then we may proceed to create the appropriate wineskin that fits our calling, gifting and cultural context.

Following what we have already said in our Clarifying Comments section of the book, we wish to further explicate and illustrate what we mean.

Life consists of polarities (tensions or opposites) and there is then a dialectical reality to life. For every thesis there is an antithesis, and both sit in creative tension with each other. Removing or emphasizing one polarity over the other would not resolve the tension but only leave one side or aspect of life, leaving the whole incomplete. The creative tension that exists between the thesis and antithesis is analogous to the arrangement of the strings of a guitar. Each string is necessary to create music according to the guitars' full capacity. The strings, like life, theology and even the Church, must be tuned to the proper key, allowing each string to exist in tension, contributing to the fullness of the music. The goal is not sameness; but fullness, for it is only in the contrast and tension that we find the music.

The method described here is dialectical, seeking to synthesize two polarities. In synthesizing we do not mean to blend both the thesis and antithesis together to come up with a combination between the two that would make each polarity something less. Such blending would produce sameness, a rather "vanilla" approach to life, the result being similar combinations with minimal variance. All human beings have DNA, and the fullness of the human race based on our genetic code, personality, development and environment is not sameness. Rather it is in a mosaic of diversity clearly featuring our Creator's brilliance and capacity. In a similar way the Church should express our Creator's brilliance and creativity, allowing for fullness as the strings are given freedom to be tuned to the proper key.

Our interest in utilizing the dialectic is for creating a framework that will allow us to focus on the reality of life, involving tension as when magnets that are seeking to attract when actually repel when like poles are placed near each other.

Having said all that, we are pressing for fullness and not "synthesis".

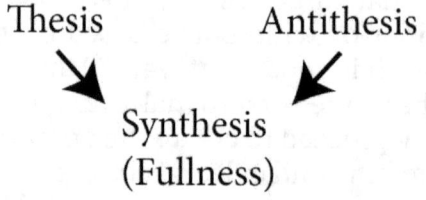

Our use of dialectic does not imply that truth is always a mixture of two sets of postulates that sit in diametric opposition. Rather, it affirms that truth is often somewhere between the extremes, in a tension that allows for the fullness of the truth to be known.

Opposite poles exist in our human experience, such as the delightful tension exhibited by the male and female of our species so wonderfully illustrates. The polarities, the provide color, spic and fullness in what would be a rather black and white, tasteless, empty life.

It is apparent that our theology, and more specifically our ecclesiology, tends to focus on one polarity at the expense of the other. For example, God is often reduced to a "cosmic principle" or a power source on one end, or a lonely father who will do anything for a relationship with His creation, on the other end of the continuum. One camp emphasizes the polarity of God's holiness; the other seeks to make God's love its total focus. Both polarities are necessary and right, but in and of themselves, leave us shy of knowing the real God as manifested in Jesus Christ (See *New Testament Trilogy*, pp. 61-62).

The continuum we are employing will help us understand the fullness of the Church as it has been expressed in our diverse, charismatic, dynamic, static, and tensioned filled history. It will allow a larger perspective in our church planting that will hopefully facilitate the fullness of God's purpose and will in your life. It will help you locate yourself on the continuum so that you will be aware of your biases, preferences, presuppositions and the like, all to help you define the kind of church you will plant.

The original basis of the Continuum of Community (our term) came from Howard A. Snyder's excellent book, *Decoding The Church: Mapping The DNA of the Christ's Body*. We were deeply enriched by Snyder's insights and appreciated deeply his "A

Broader Perspective" section (pp. 21-23) in which he unpacked the "four classic marks" of the Church as found in The Nicene Creed which states "We believe in **one holy catholic** and **apostolic** Church." The four marks being *one, holy, catholic* and *apostolic*. Snyder's contention is that these four marks were often interpreted, or reinterpreted, or even harmonized with various systems of thought and then applied accordingly. Snyder believes the four marks are essentially one polarity that is lacking unless another polarity is provided. He the sets the polarities between what he calls the "Organic Movement" and the "Organized Institution." He charts these as follows (*Decoding The Church*, p. 23):

Organic Movement	**Organized Institution**
Diverse, Varied	One, Uniform
Charismatic	Holy (sacred)
Local, Contextual	Catholic, Universal
Prophetic Word	Apostolic Authority

Snyder boldly asserts:

Classic theology has tended to speak of one holy catholic and apostolic church. Less frequently has it spoken of the church as diverse, charismatic, local, and prophetic. Yet if we take our ecclesiological cues from the Book of Acts, or even the Gospels, we see it is the second set of qualities that often is emphasized...DNA is always made up of four base pairs of compounds. The components of each pair are not opposites but are complementary. Likewise, the contrasting sets of marks of the church that we have discussed are not in opposition to each other but are instead complementary (Decoding The Church, p. 22)

We wholeheartedly agree and give a resounding "amen" to his statement. It is "both/and".

This aspect of fullness which Snyder calls *"complimentary"* is precisely what we are seeking to establish. It is a "both/and" approach which allows the tensions to co-exist, resulting in more, not less. Less is the natural by product when one polarity is emphasized over another, or even excluded all together. Our only concern in Snyder's continuum is that he seems to inadvertently set "Organic" in contrast to "Organized", which will work as *complimentary* polarities. However, if one is seeking to find fullness as a result of "Organic" and "Organized" then something more than these two polarities needs to exist. Snyder is utilizing his continuum more as a complementary, DNA compound pair, and in that regard his usage is excellent. However, if we place the complementary pair into a continuum and press for fullness then the polarities of "organic" and "organized" lack the necessary tension required for fullness to occur. We are missing some guitar strings, and our music is incomplete. The tensions do not seem broad enough to encompass the reality of life and the history of the Church. That is, if we believe the Church is a living organism then much like the human body, it would require both structure (skeletal frame or framework, the Nicene Creed), or what we call "static," and the more free flowing dynamic elements of the human make up (personality, emotions, will, etc.) which we call, "dynamic," the diverse, charismatic, local, and prophetic. The polarities would then be "static" and "dynamic" with fullness being "organic". It only seems apparent to us that the fullness we are seeking is life or what we are calling "organic," something alive like a human being. Such a living organism would include more resilient, static elements set in tension with elements of the polarity we call dynamic.

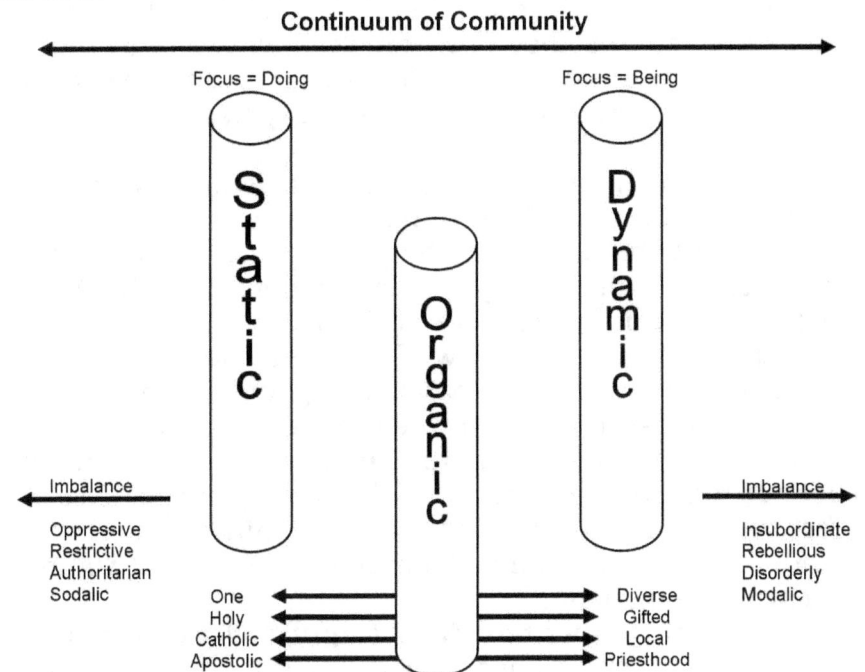

Continuum of Community

Static: One, holy, catholic, apostolic (Focus: Doing)
Dynamic: Diverse, gifted, local, priesthood (Focus: Being)
Organic: Fullness of both (Community)

Historically, within the Church we have witnessed the extremes in every capacity. For our purpose here we will look at the polarities of our organizational constructs. The **Continuum of Community** reveals that the two polarities in tension with each other are static and dynamic. The static would be those organizational structures such as the historic Christian faith (the creeds of old such as the Nicene and Apostle's Creed), mainline denominations, etc. Static is not a negative term but simply a description of one polarity as is "dynamic" of the other.

The **static** is then the historic Christian faith being passed on from one generation to the next through the "one, holy, catholic, and apostolic" church. The **"dynamic"** is then the historic Christian faith being passed expressed in any given generation, and passed on to the next, through the "diverse, gifted, local, and priesthood". We are dealing with two aspects of the same organism, the skeletal framework and the personality. Together they are **the fullness of God's expression** through the Church (Ephesians 1:23).

This combination of *being* and *doing* is the essence of the Church as a community. The Church is a living organism wherein activity is not the key to life but the by product or result of it, more simply, the activity of life flowing from life. Another way of saying this is what we do flows from who we are, so, what a church does (doing) flows from the identity (being) of the church. One cannot really separate being and doing but here it allows us to illustrate and capture the thought that organic life has a natural flow and process to it. It must be birthed, nurtured, facilitated (environment – more on this later) and released as well as fostered, connected, organized and maintained. Church is then meant to be organic and living, necessitating the "Both/And" for fullness to be experienced.

The church is then both **"one"** (unity) and **"diverse"** (many). We are one church, unified because of Christ, and yet many churches expressing this unity in radical and creative diversity, manifesting, at least in part, the creative fullness of our God.

The church is both **"holy"** (set apart, sacred) and **"gifted"** (grace empowered). Both are the work of the Holy Spirit. The Church is then set apart for the glory of God as "holy" and sacred; a community or "holy" Kingdom for a holy King. Snyder implies that the "holy" is the fruit of the Spirit, the character of Christ. On the other hand, the Church is "gifted" for the express purpose of glorifying the King through the manifold "gifts of the Spirit" that allow the Church to carry out its function and mission in the world. Snyder equates this with the charisma of Jesus.

The church is **"catholic"** (universal) and **"local"** (locally expressed in your cultural context, e.g., town). We are one "catholic" (as understood as it was originally meant) or "universal" church transcendent of culture and yet, many churches locally expressed within a specific culture. In this sense, "the church both transcends culture and immerses itself in particular cultures" (Howard A. Snyder, *Decoding The Church*, p. 25). The Church throughout history has tended to struggle with this aspect of fullness, most often focusing on "uniformity over particularity, universality over locality, cultural transcendence over cultural incarnation, and stability and predictability over innovation." (Snyder, p. 25)

The church is both **"apostolic"** (based on the gospel passed on through apostles) and **"priesthood"** (every believer a priest). The foundation of our faith rests on the apostolic message "that Christ died for our sins, just as the Scriptures said. He was buried, and he was raised from the dead on the third day" (I Corinthians 15:3-4). The Church is then built upon the foundation of the apostles and prophets (Ephesians 2:20), the apostolic message declared for all time and the prophetic word spoken for a particular time. However the Church also finds its foundation in the "priesthood of all believers" (I Peter 2:9; Revelation 1:6), where each individual carries on the apostolic tradition that has been passed down, declaring the message for all time, and the prophetic, declaring the message for a particular time.

Extremes of "Static" Pole

When something moves to an extreme in either of the polarities, the health and focus of the organism shifts, resulting in chaos, sickness, functioning far below the parameters of its creation, and even death. Here are some extremes of the "static" pole.

Oppressive: The needs and demands of the organization reign supreme over the mission and the community, fostering oppression wherein the needs of the few, particularly the one, outweigh the needs of the many.

Restrictive: As the organization grows it becomes ever more limited in its scope, gradually moving from mission to maintenance focus, and requiring more commitment and restriction of its members to fulfill the requirements of membership. The guidelines that once formed the church become the "bounded set" of rules required for life maintenance, instead of being the result of life being lived.

Authoritarian: The focus is not on giving away authority and power and developing people, but on the preservation of power and the structure that enforce it, of course, in the name of mission.

Sodalic bias: The sodalic bias is not wrong per se, but incomplete without a modalic bias to insure fullness. Sodality deals with the organization, the fellowship and the doing of ministry. In this imbalance, one gets swallowed up in the belly of the beast. In other words, the needs, the demands and maintenance requirements of the organization (all good and necessary) eventually drive the church more than does the mission. The mission becomes the maintenance of the organization, or the beast. Oddly enough, churches can begin as a fellowship, a community, only to become a fellowship/organization that while trying to be a fellowship unfortunately begins to use people as a means to an end. Ironically the mission of loving God, loving others and making disciples gets lost in the demands of the beast, creating an environment in which humanity is sacrificed for the artificial life of the organization.

Extremes of The "Dynamic" Pole

The "dynamic" pole provides fullness as form does to function. However, with extremes, we are talking about how the church or individuals have historically reacted to the extremes of the "static" pole. When there is an over emphasis on structure, authority, rules and the organization it is only logical that when one breaks away from such an institution one would react and create something that would emphasize the polar opposites. The extremes of the dynamic pole are precisely those polar opposites.

Insubordinate: Because of the personal and individual nature of the "dynamic" pole (focus on being), a sense of insubordination tends to arise. Due to the restrictive, oppressive and authoritarian imbalances of the static pole, when an individual stands against this oppression and pursues and finds freedom, he or she rejects that authority, indeed, very often any kind of authority. It is precisely this non-submission to people and to a mission that sets in motion a spreading insubordination, a virus passed on to others. This is largely due to the focus having shifted from the whole, the organization, to the one, the organism. Herein individuals tend to believe they matter more than the whole. Submission is only to the mission and Jesus and not to the leaders or people. This virus is damaging to the spiritual DNA, which once encoded in those who start movements, will find that their children or disciples grow up to be just like them, insubordinate. Everything reproduces according to its kind, and what is sown in corruptibility will be corrupt.

Rebellious: The dynamic pole tends to create an environment that rebels against itself because of its emphasis on personal freedom at the expense of corporate solidarity. If a church leader **responds** to the extremes of the static pole in a way that seeks fullness we will likely see the birth of a healthy church and movement. However, if the leader **reacts** to the extremes of the static pole, rejecting it and swinging to the other extreme, we will likely see the birth of a rebellious and reactionary church, one that is the antithesis of the static polarity.

Disorderly: The extreme here is a direct result of the church placing its emphasis more on its state of being, on a community leadership style where all decide, resisting a hierarchy of leaders or attempting to lead from a relational perspective that highlights the person and the personal. Because of the over emphasis on the form or state of being, the church struggles to maintain itself because there is no, or very little, thought given to the structure that could maintain and even multiply the church. Since relationship with God and others, the state of being, is all that matters very little time is spent on the structural realities that would encourage, enhance and multiply this state of being.

Modalic bias: The state of being is critical, and if neglected, leads to sterility and even death. The dynamic pole is not in danger of neglecting this, but in danger of over emphasizing it because it focuses more on being than on doing. The heart and soul of this imbalance is the belief that the "way" they do things is vital and necessary, to the extreme neglect of establishing functional structures, or in some cases any structures.

How one avoids the extremes is a delicate process. In one sense, it is true that human nature will seek homeostasis, or equilibrium of some sort; which means that over time the church will harden in its structure no matter how static or dynamic you seek to be. This stability will, over time, harden and some sense of revitalization will become necessary. One cannot avoid the extremes if one does not embrace the fullness, the "both/and" reality of the Church.

The goal is then to avoid the extremes of the polarities, embracing the fullness of a "both/and" approach. The goal is not balance but fullness. It can be said that balance is a lie. The reason is that to have balance you to be in control. If you are after balance, that becomes the focus, resulting in sterility, structural rigidity, and restriction instead of freedom, flexibility, and on going growth and multiplication adjusting to the life and cultural dynamics. You compromise all things to achieve one thing, balance. As you exercise control you must by definition exclude something. **To embrace the organic fullness of "both/and" you must embrace both the static elements of the Church and the dynamic elements as well,** not in some sort of compromise, but in totality. You cannot exclude one polarity and cling to another, or try to straddle both and "balance" between the two. What this full embrace will look like from one planter to another, among cultures, in various movements, in different places will be beautifully varied and diverse.

As a church planter you must locate yourself on the continuum so that you can become aware of the particular biases and preferences you have for church. That is: Do you currently prefer structure or not, prefer form over function or not, prefer being over doing, or not? Do you tend to be all about the mission without regard for relationship, or be all about the relationship and forget the mission, etc? From there you can begin to map your pathway to fullness.

For some of you locating yourself on the continuum will take some time as you will need to sort through, identify and release the hurts you have experienced in your previous church experiences; because you will have a tendency to want to plant a church in direct contrast to your negative church experiences.

The best way to constantly press for fullness in your church is to recognize your gifting and human limitation, accept both and then locate yourself on the Continuum of Community, acknowledging the strengths of your location as well as the inherent weaknesses. From that point you will want to build in a constant assessment and adjustment process in the life of your church through prayer, community dialogue with your leadership, and various assessment tools. You will need to determine where your church exists and functions within the static and dynamic polarities. The path to fullness has many course corrections, and you will embrace a continual dynamic of fluidity and change, all based on the static on the centrality of who Jesus has called you to be and what He has called you to do. There will be many such course corrections in the life of your church. We encourage you to incorporate this process of evaluation for fullness early into the life of your new church.

Keep in mind that it is not so vital that a particular process or way of assessing be implemented, although one might be better than another. We are encouraging you simply to have something of a process. As we have stated, fullness must "both/and." In other words, churches that experience fullness will not look, worship or act the same. Healthy human bodies do not all look the same or act the same although they have many things in common. The way life is expressed and lived out results in a beautiful tapestry or mosaic that resembles the heart of our God. So, the evaluation you use should not be a model from another church, or someone else's fruit in ministry, but on what embracing static and dynamic looks like for you.

We return to our original question: "What kind of church am I going to plant?" Let's now take a look at our cultural situation.

Church Planting in the Post-Christian West

We live in a society that is quickly and constantly changing. The Judeo-Christian ethic is no longer the guiding norm of our lives, spirituality in various forms is a real pursuit for many. The "uni" in universe is non-existent – we are now many "verses" in a continuum that lacks an absolute force that keeps all the "verses" unified or together. The Church in the West, in its present form, no longer appeals or relates to an ever increasing number of our population. There is a quiet resistance to Christianity in the West, as it is the one religion that is carefully singled out and marginalized. As tolerance for all religions is being espoused and endorsed, Christianity is quietly attacked, sidelined and muzzled. (In some cases, maybe we deserve the muzzle). Our point here is not to engage in a cultural dialogue, or to create an "us" versus "them" mentality, but to recognize the state of our world in the West. We can see the spiritual hunger and need. Spirituality is accepted in our land, and our country is hungry for something more. What is rejected is the current incarnation of the Church. This provides us a great opportunity to live out the gospel to a world looking for a solution to its ever-increasing sense of cosmic aloneness and purposeless existence. Our churches might actually grow in impact and force if we are simply good Christians first and foremost. Just a thought for your marketing campaign: Grow authentic Christians and your church might grow too.

Postmodernism Made Simple

There have been myriad books written about the postmodern shift we have encountered. We will not engage in the dialogue here other than to say a few simple things about the state of our current universe, or maybe disassociated collection of "verses." Or whatever. As we noted earlier, there really is no "uni" in our universe any more. We are not a universe but a collection of verses that are a part of the cosmic whole, which in turn, lacks an absolute force that keeps all the "verses" together. We no longer have a center for our existence or reality. We are now a "dis-centered" or "un-centered" people.

A major characteristic of our age can be summed up in one word -- centerless. There is now no clear center that unites the ever increasing, divergent, elements of our world. There is no common standard to which societies and people can turn in their attempts to judge or value ideas, opinions, lifestyles, or even religious ideologies. The once commonly agreed-upon base of authority in the modernistic age is now a historic footnote in the archives of human history. It is obvious that this shift to a center-less world has resulted in a conglomeration of fragmented societies, told as local or individual narratives. A world without a center does free one from the abusive power that can bring bondage and limit human freedom and expression, but it also leaves the human soul without a place to anchor itself for a sense of security.

In our postmodern world there is really no "world" in "worldview," or the thought of absolute truth. We now live in a world where there is no metanarrative, no over-arching story that defines and interprets reality. There is no one tale, one accepted norm, which governs our understanding of reality absolutely and in finality. Our society has rejected the metanarrative, no longer believing that one system or narrative can bring humanity together into one global people and community. Instead of the metanarrative we now have local, even individual, narratives whose parameters lie within the confines and context of the societies in which people live. More simply stated, the local narratives are constructed within a societal or communal framework, and help construct and interpret reality. The exciting element about this for church planters is the societal or communal thrust of our postmodern shift. Our world is moving ever more to a relational emphasis that is seeking to make sense of life by sharing it with others. The hit comedy "Friends" exemplified this masterfully and in a most entertaining way as the six characters seek to understand themselves in relation to each other, which in turn, allowed them understand who they were in relation to the world. They do all this by allowing each to discover the truth without forcing their views upon one another, individual/local narratives coming together to form a community wherein the newly created community then interprets and re-interprets reality for each of them.

In the modernistic world, meaning was defined by a few. We are now in a world where meaning is shared and interpreted by the many, which fostering the belief that if nothing is really "out there" that defines us, then we are left with is nothing but interpretation and co-existence with other human beings and our planet. The focus becomes less on the "what" of our existence, but rather on the "how" of life. That is, since we really cannot know the absolute, because it varies for each societal network, then what we are left with is how we will interpret what is, and live accordingly.

From all this we can say that our postmodern culture can be simply defined as a being without hope, without purpose, and is internally disconnected. If we are now nothing more than random accidents in the mystery of some cosmic explosion of the galactic expanse, nothing more than local narratives with no sense of an absolute governing our existence, then it is understandable why so many people find their lives without hope. Having such a view of reality tends to foster cynicism and pessimism. If we are nothing more than the accidental assimilation of atoms that somehow over time organized themselves into matter that we now call a human being, it is no wonder we are living without purpose. The "why" of life is still left nagging at us, reminding us that there has to be something more than this. If this is the case then no wonder people feel so disconnected. The postmodern generation needs hope, purpose, and connection, and the Church is in a perfect position to provide that, if we live out the two great relationships of loving God and loving others and follow our mission of making disciples. The answers to life are resolved in relationship with God, the human longing of connectedness finds relief in the two great relationships, and in the ever demanding need for purpose. This condition of despair finds relief in the loving reality of fellowship with the community of the Trinity, the community of the faithful called the Church, and in the fulfillment of the mission of making disciples.

Dr. Robert Webber helps us understand this a little more clearly as he provides this thoughtful insight. "Christians in the postmodern world will succeed, not by watering down the faith, but by being a counter-cultural community that invites people to be shaped by the story of Israel and Jesus." A local narrative lived out within a community that submits to and loves the Ultimate Community, God as Trinity.

Counter Cultural Thoughts

Being counter-cultural is no easy matter. It is hard to be a person who loves those who are full of hate and evil. The choice of retreating and building a Christian culture in protected isolation is much easier. We may not go the full Amish route of retreat, but a slight variation of such does seem appealing. After all, it's very hard to keep pure in this world. How do we keep our children from engaging in evil without allowing them the safety of retreat? What does it mean to be in the world but not of it? Aren't we supposed to hate sin? Hard questions, and this chapter will not provide an adequate answer. Instead of providing an answer, we wish to pose some questions.

There is so much talk in our Christian culture about "avoiding the appearance of evil," which translated often means staying away from anything and anyone that is evil. The definition of evil is subjective and interpreted individually by each believer and the verse is oddly utilized in various situations and seems to be nothing more than a statement of preference. Exactly what is evil? If we are applying the biblical definition, the entire world is. After all, it is anti-God, full of self and engaged in a conspiracy that is led by Lucifer himself. If we are going to avoid the appearance of evil, then maybe we should pack up and retreat as the Amish?

Who do we boycott? What do we allow or disallow? Just how tightly do we close our eyes and ears to the cries of the world?

Is it wrong to have friends who do not know Christ? If we are to avoid everything that is evil, then should we stop reading the Bible because it contains scenes of rape, drunkenness, witchcraft, murder, lust and sex? How far do we take this? Are we even asking the right questions? If so, then Jesus violated this very command of Paul by associating with those who were evil. As a result, He was indicted as being a drunkard and a glutton (Matthew 11:19). We are grateful He associated out with sinners and loved them. As far as we know, we are in the camp of those evil sinners He was willing to sit with. The pure Son of God was so pure that He could love someone like us. Maybe that is the question we should be asking? Are we so pure in our lives that we look nothing like Jesus? We worry far too much about how much sin might get in and not enough about how much love might get out, all thoughts for your newly forming church to consider.

Maybe the question is not how do we avoid evil or how much evil do we avoid? Rather, how do we love and serve a broken and lost generation? Evangelical Christianity is often far too concerned about power and position: how to get it and how to use it for personal gain or furthering a political agenda. We somehow think that is the opposite of what Jesus is all about. The primary question believers should be asking is "What can I do to serve you?"

The gospel is not about getting saved and isolating. It is about a God who came to a sinful world. No matter how hard you try to be neat, changing diapers is a messy business. Dealing with sin and sinful people is no different. The wise sage of Proverbs tells us that "an empty stable stays clean." (NLT) There is no question that life is much more defined, predictable and even safe when we disallow sinners into the mix. Scripture does not tell us to keep the stable clean, but to keep our hearts pure. And one of the characteristics of a pure heart is its willingness to change diapers. We can't transform culture until we find ourselves transformed. Jesus said it this way:

> *Woe to you, teachers of the law and Pharisees, you hypocrites! You clean the outside of the cup and dish, but inside they are full of greed and self-indulgence. Blind Pharisee! First clean the inside of the cup and dish, and then the outside also will be clean. (Matthew 23:25-26)*

The life of faith is not about judgment and withdrawal from an evil society. It is about engagement and sacrifice – something like taking up your cross and letting your light shine in such a way that all might see your good deeds and give praise to our Father who is in heaven (Matt. 5:16).

"What Are You Going To Do To Me?"

During a coaching appointment with a church planter and his wife, Mike was enjoying the fellowship and enthusiasm the couple brought. After all, talking with church planters, people pregnant with new life is a delight as they ponder and dream about this new life that is forming in them.

Mike asked them about their church and what it would be like. They immediately answered with exuberance as the husband began to unpack what the Sunday morning service would look like. It is always amazing how a church planter will immediately default to the description of the Sunday morning service when you ask them about the church. He described in thoughtful detail what the worship service would consist of, smiling and leaning forward as he explained how their service will have excellent worship. With their creative arts background, they will utilize drama to illustrate life and the gospel, the preaching will be relational, and the texture of the services will be one of community and family helping people grow in Christ. All of it sounded great but didn't answer the question Mike was really asking.

Mike listened and then with quiet intensity asked the question that sent both the husband and wife back in their seats. Mike went on to say, "I have just come to your church with my wife and children. What will you do to me and my family that would cause us to come back to your church?" In other words, "Who are you and how will your story and the story of God impact my life and my family?"

Mike then went on to encourage the enthusiastic couple. He deeply appreciated the thought they had put behind the worship service, but he wanted them to think a little further and deal with the what kind of community or people they were going to be, not just what kind of service they were going to do.

The passion and values were already resident in the couple,

and after a few minutes they passionately shared what they would to do Mike and his family. With great precision and heart they began to describe the kind of church they wanted to be, and not just the personality or style they wanted to employ.

The default position of our churches in the West tends to be to focus on the public service which generally meets on Sunday mornings. It appears by the answer of most church planters we have heard over the years that the public venue is the major and sometimes only focus of the church. In reality, ministering to the crowds is vital and significant, but the real goal is to develop the people into followers of Christ and a community of the faithful that share life and love of Jesus with each other and the world around them. Sunday morning church services alone won't accomplish this.

"What kind of Church will you be?" Whatever wineskin you create for your church based on your calling, gifting and cultural context it is important that you are a Church that helps people love God, love each other and, as they live life together, makes disciples and does this all together as a community of the faithful.

R.E.A.D. Questions

Each chapter in this book will have a series of questions. Using the acronym R.E.A.D., these questions will help you **R**eflect, **E**valuate, **A**djust and **D**o.

Wisdom in the Holy Spirit comes from reflecting on biblical truth. Evaluation allows you to look at your current ministry praxis in light of a biblical world view. This allows you to adjust your life and ministry accordingly (read, repent).

The questions at the end of each chapter are framed within the context of applied theology (theology that seeks to live out what it knows) which encompasses every aspect of our life - our identity, capacity and destiny in Christ. However, we will use an artificial construct of "life and ministry practice" to help you self-evaluate within the broader, prevalent, thinking in the Western Church. Prayerfully reflect upon each question and allow the Holy Spirit to nourish your soul and establish a base of wisdom that will allow you to navigate through the tumultuous waters of ecclesiological life.

Chapter One R.E.A.D. Questions - "So, You Want To Plant A Church?"

R -

- Based on your *reflection*, list the three major things that the Holy Spirit spoke to your heart regarding your church plant.
- *Reflect* on why you want to plant a church and what kind of church you will plant.
- Given our postmodern culture, *reflect* on the issues our current cultural situation creates for you.
- Describe your most recent personal encounter with God. How is this encounter impacting your church plant?

E -

- Based on the new awareness that you have gained, how would you *evaluate* your current life and church plant?
- *Evaluate* how your church plant will address the cultural issues of our day.
- Based on your location in the Continuum of Community, evaluate the strengths and weaknesses of your current biases and presuppositions about the Church.

A -

What do you need to *adjust* on each of the above?

D -

What will you *do* about it?

PART 1 - DNA FORMATION

CHAPTER 2 - WHO ARE YOU?

There is the classic story about the business travelers stuck in a snow storm at O'Hare international Airport in Chicago, and the harried counter agent trying to book dozens of frustrated travelers on the first flight out. A man approached the podium, cutting ahead in line, demanding to be cared for right away. When told he would have to go get back in line, he pressured the agent, forcefully saying, "Do you know who I am?" The agent picked up the public address microphone at the podium, and accessing the general address system, said, "May I have your attention please? We have a gentleman who seems to have forgotten who he is. If there is anyone can help him discover his identity, please help the poor man out." The cranky passenger realized he had been bested, and sheepishly went to the end of the line, all to the sound of the approving applause of the crowd.

Like the frustrated traveler, we too, need someone to tell us who we are. Before we can begin any journey with Christ, any partnership with Him in a church planting endeavor, we must first know who He is and who we are in Him. Why is this self-understanding important to you as a church planter? There are many reasons, and we will discuss them as we go through this chapter. However, one major factor is that ministry in the post-Christian era we live in is defined by two things - *relationships and story.* People want to know who you are, what your story is - not just what you believe. They aren't interested in your quest, your plan to start this church, but they are interested in your life's journey. Knowing who we are in Christ allows us to be secure, and relate to people in live-giving ways. Such self-awareness also empowers us to tell our story to other people, without fear and false humility, in a way that can help them see Jesus at work in us, and through us. Knowing who we are is essential to our ministry fruitfulness in our culture today.

If we look at the totality of who we are in Christ, we see the emergence of a sphere of being that comprises the various aspects of who we are. The term "sphere" is used to convey an understanding of each life aspect, which is all encompassing and three dimensional, implying the boundaries and definition of a subject.

There is a **personal-life sphere** that circumscribes that which forms a biblical framework for our individual spiritual existence, namely our **Identity**, our **Capacity**, and our **Destiny**.

Personal Life Sphere

In our **identity**, we are Sons and Daughters of the Most High God. We are born into His family, restored in the Imago Dei. Sons and daughters of a King are known as princes and princesses. Being born into the family of God is the restoration of our identity as princes and princesses.

In our character we are being developed to be Servants - an attitude of heart that determines our **capacity** to fulfill the God-given destiny we each have. Our **destiny** is to be a Steward in God's house which is our role in the "family business".

Identity: We are Sons and Daughters as We are Born Into a Family

To those who accept Jesus as Christ He gives the right/power to become children of God, born not of a human will, but born anew by God (John 1:12-13). Our sonship and daughtership comes with a spiritual genetic code from our Father in the person of the Holy Spirit. The Spirit brings Christ-likeness to us, and joins us at the heart with others in the family of God. We are being renewed in the knowledge of the Imago Dei (Colossians 3:10) which has been imprinted upon us. And, like little ducklings following after their mother, we find ourselves pursuing, God wanting to go where He goes and be like Him. This forms the core of our spiritual self-image fashioned in the crucible of relationship with God. We, as the sons and daughters of Adam, are created in His image. We find ourselves marred at birth by the fallen nature of this world, and then afforded the redeeming privilege in Christ to be renewed inwardly into His image. Our community, the other ducklings, also helps us form our identity as we relate with each other, discovering that they have the same genetics as we do, and together we learn about our Parent.

Image is the key to identity, that self-concept or picture everyone has within that reveals who they are and how much inherent value they believe they possess or do not possess. Identity is the key to all human interactions as we can only relate and find fulfillment as human beings, not human doings. As a result, identity is the key to successful discipleship. What is encoded in us and imprinted upon us, by the Spirit of God through regeneration and by those around us through shared life in the redeemed community, is the foundation of our identity in Christ. How deeply our sonship (daughterhood is assumed when we say this) is set in our self-perception and, if we are growing in our understanding of this reality, determines whether we will be fruitful in our walk with the Lord. This identity perception as a child of God will determine if we will overcome the challenges of this life.

Jesus knew who He was - the Son of the Father. His certainty about His identity allowed Him to face all challenges and tests presented to Him without failing one. We can only know who we are when we know Whose we are. Indeed, the pursuit of understanding our sonship in Christ is quite possibly the most vital issue of the Christian life, as so much of how we walk in this life is determined by the right apprehension of this understanding.

Identity is the backbone of our character, allowing us to stand in the day of evil. Much has been written on how the Lord uses His Spirit and the written Word, the Bible, to form identity in us. Not much has been written, at least of late, about how the Kingdom community - that shared life together in Christ - is used by God to form identity. The reflection of Christ, His nature, the fullness of His grace, is seen only in His Body. Only He had the capacity to retain the fullness of God (Colossians 1:19), so now such fullness must be expressed in and through His Body.

Growing up with others of like genetics influences the development of our identity. We learn about who we are from our family. Any child locked away from other human beings will not be likely to develop a normal self-perception. Any Christian locked away from God's community will not develop a proper understanding of sonship. As discussed, the cultural ideal of the self-reliant, individualistic person who is totally self-sufficient stands in opposition to this thought. We are taught we can be complete without any other person. We are imprinted with such things as "stand on your own two feet," "go it alone," "make YOUR mark on the world," and "you can do it!" (And of course, we men are taught to never stop and ask directions!) The thought of being interdependent with others, that we actually need others and what they offer us in their persons, is a cultural anathema. Saying that who we are as a person is, in part, the direct result of the shaping influence brought by the lives of others, has an effect on us like to that of fingernails dragged across a chalk-board! It grates on us and makes us cringe.

We find, in the early pages of the Scripture, God talking about creation with great joy as the text says over and over that "God saw that it was good," and with the culmination of man and woman, "it is very good." What then stands out is the line in chapter 2 verse 18 where God says, "It is not good for the man to be alone." Amid all the descriptions of creation as good, we come across the first description that tells us what is not good. What a powerful picture this is for us to ponder that the divine design of the human race is based upon the image of the Creator which is relational. Our very need for each other has been given by God. Yes we subvert it and render the order backward at times, but the desire for the other is still from God and right. The Church is then a powerful expression of that life shared and lived together as an interdependent community.

Yet the New Testament has clear examples of how God's character, nature and His ways were demonstrated to, and imparted to, one person by the example of others with whom they lived community. As we have said, Jesus did this as His primary method of developing His disciples. Paul reminded Timothy to reflect on Paul's pursuit of Christ - his life and teaching, and sent Timothy as an example of that way of life to the Christians in Corinth (1 Corinthians 4:15-17).

Our acceptance by the members of our community, our family, the Church is an important part of understanding our intrinsic value as recreated in the image of God (Romans 15:7). Such acceptance is essential in forming the proper self-worth understanding from God's perspective - not proud and puffed up and not degraded and broken down (Romans 12:3).

Healthy self-awareness is a key component to a properly

formed identity. Rejection, with which our world is filled, brings the opposite. So, life in community brings a demonstration of God's love and acceptance that is critical in the formation of one's identity as a disciple, and even healing from the wounds we may have received from being rejected by others. We have all been hurt by human beings, a bad relationship for example. If we have been hurt by, a person then the only way we can find healing is through a person. Healing then comes through the medium of relationship: that is a relationship with God and a relationship with another. How perfectly the Church is set up to be that agency or place, where people find their hearts healed, discover their purpose of existence and find love, value and acceptance for who they are as human beings created in the Image of God.

Another way that community forms and informs the development of our identity is by giving us a sense of belonging. It is similar to the affect of acceptance, but goes beyond that into seeing one's self as part of a larger whole. Acceptance allows us to belong; to what we belong to becomes part of who we are. Having a sense of belonging to something larger than ourselves defines us. It also inspires us to pursue growth as a person. A passion to grow, fueled by having the first elements of self-definition provided by the larger context, all but assures that any further growth will follow the same pattern provided by that context. We will become more of what we already are, more of what our environment is - just deeper, fuller, more mature and complete in its pattern. The track is set, the train will run on it until something of equal significance brings influence, and as a consequence, a possible change of direction.

This is how the Church as community influences the development of our identity. We are designed for relationship ("I/Thou"), and genetically encoded spiritually by the Trinity to only be most completed as part of a larger whole:

> *But you are a chosen people, a royal priesthood, a holy nation, a people belonging to God, that you may declare the praises of him who called you out of darkness into his wonderful light. Once you were not a people, but now you are the people of God; once you had not received mercy, but now you have received mercy. (1 Peter 2:9-10)*

We are not chosen persons, but a chosen people. We are not

individually priests, but a royal priesthood. We are not persons belonging to God, we are a people belonging to God. The "you" of the New Testament Church is plural. We are these things collectively, we are these things together. We are a spiritual nation, not a spiritual isolation.

Belonging to a community which accepts us, that is the living incarnation of Christ's Body, which is living out its priesthood, living as a representative people for God - not just in words pledging to do so, but in practical works - being part of this kind of community cannot help but shape our identity as individuals. The life, the nature of the larger group, its ways and insights, its values, doctrine and methods of spiritual practice, all become part of the individual. The environment ennobles: the larger context of a shared life informs and defines who we are, and who we become. This understanding of I/Thou is detailed more specifically in the graph below.

I/Thou Model

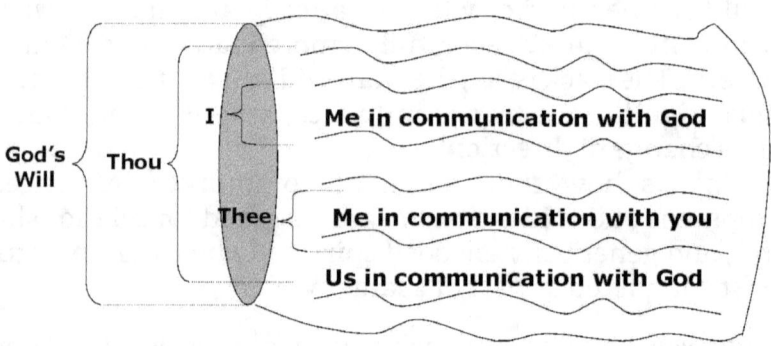

Life Received/Life Given = As I've been Embraced by God (Being with God), I now Embrace others (Being With Others) and share the life of Jesus with my world (Being For Others).

As church planters, we must have a solid understanding of our identity, who we are in Christ as a son or daughter, as this understanding is what will serve as the foundation for our ministry. Likewise, understanding the community of Christ from which this plant will be birthed and the members of the core community of this church plant are both essential. Understanding these relationships, and how they inform your identity as a church planter, are key in understanding yourself as the leader of this quest. ***What you do in Christ proceeds from who you are in Christ.*** Knowing who you are is the foundation of knowing what to do.

Capacity: We are Servants Who are Being Developed in Our Hearts

As we enter the next phase of our discussion of the personal-life sphere of a Christian, it is quite possible for one to misunderstand what we are about to say here concerning capacity and confuse it with the idea of ability. Therefore, we will seek to define it, and draw distinction up front. Capacity is related to ability, but is distinct from it. While ability is the power to do something, to perform some task, like a carpenter has the ability to build a house, capacity is what allows us to "learn" how to do a thing, the aptitude for something, and consequently is the foundation of all skills. Someone who does not have the capacity (e.g. required level of mental faculties, manual dexterity) can never learn how to be a carpenter, and, therefore, cannot have the capacity to build a house. They might have the mental ability to envision the house and do the math, but they might not be able to drive a nail. Or, they might be a wiz with tools, but never be able to see how it all comes together. The mental wiring and physical gifting they were endowed with, their capacity, will determine their ability.

In the spiritual context, capacity speaks of our nature, our character, our heart. That's why in the qualifications for Elders (in I Timothy 3) are capacities of being, rather than abilities for doing. Only one is a competency - "able to teach" - and even this one will collapse if the other character qualities are not present.

The key to unleashing our God-given capacity is to take on the servant attitude of Christ Jesus (Philippians 2:1-11). The attitude of a servant puts to death the self and exalts the "others," the Lord and those we serve. Only servants are sons, and all sons are servants. Jesus explained this in Matthew 7:20-23:

> *Not everyone who says to me, 'Lord, Lord,' will enter the kingdom of heaven, but only he who does the will of my Father who is in heaven. Many will say to me on that day, 'Lord, Lord, did we not prophesy in your name, and in your name drive out demons and perform many miracles?' Then I will tell them plainly, 'I never knew you. Away from me, you evildoers!'*

Jesus made it clear that mere words and great works of power were not the hallmark of God's people, but rather a submissive heart, that desires to please the Father, the heart of a servant. If you are going to be effective as a planter, you must take this attitude: "I am here to serve this community and the needs of the people in it." Without this attitude, your plant will be ineffective and fruitless as far as spiritual matters are concerned.

While we will discuss **grace empowerment** at length in the next section on destiny, we must mention it he now, to connect the idea of capacity with the understanding of destiny. Even though God's enablement for service comes to us as a grace-unction of His Spirit, and therefore is unmerited, our ability to function in that empowerment (and indeed survive it) is based on our capacity. Our hearts must be truly converted, our passions under His dominion and our personal ambitions must be dead on the Cross if we hope to learn how to function most effectively in our Spiritual gifts. Expansion of the heart increases our capacity and our effectiveness within our grace empowerment. As our heart becomes more servant-motivated and less self-motivated, God is able to release more of His empowering grace to us. Without such a heart, our capacity to function most effectively within our personal, specific empowerment is diminished, and potentially fatal to what we call ministry. Church planters will be tested in their character before being released by the Holy Spirit to plant (more on this in a later section).

Such capacity in our redeemed nature, our character and its quality, is the foundation for our destiny. It is here that capacity meets ability, as our heart has been prepared as a servant to take on the task for which we were originally created, and through which we will make our ultimate contribution in God's economy. Identity has placed us in His family, capacity has placed us in His will, and destiny now places us strategically as a resource in

His cosmic undertakings. His ability to place us is related directly to what degree of faithful servanthood we have already been proven (Matthew 25:21). Where we have been tested and found faithful, we can be entrusted with more, a good principle to utilize for developing disciples and from those disciples leaders for the Kingdom.

Destiny: We are Stewards Who Have a Place of Responsibility in The "Kingdom Economy"

Our destiny can be thought of as God's plan for us to make our ultimate contribution in His Kingdom economy as He seeks to reconcile mankind to Himself. In your case, you are considering or have considered, that church planting may be part of this destiny. What He has sovereignly placed in us, what spiritual gifts and natural abilities, what opportunities He has arranged for our development, all of these are "talents" which He has invested in us, empowering us for Kingdom contribution (Matthew 25:14-30). We are stewards of this grace-investment. **It is not important how much we have been entrusted with, but with how we undertake our stewardship**. Will we be faithful, or will we squander what we have been given? Here, too, community is involved in forming our destiny. Let's unpack this.

As part of our destiny, we are stewards of many things: family, finances, etc. we will discuss the bulk of these later. The area within destiny stewardship which we wish to focus on now is the stewardship of that which we might call our ministry. The term "ministry" can be such a charged term, meaning so many different things to various people. We have been using it here as meaning the individual's contribution, as part of the large whole of the Church, to God's Kingdom economy as He works reconciliation with mankind. Specifically for you, church planting is how you have considered working this out. This, too, is formed and informed by the larger community. For the purposes of our discussion, we will look at two elements of ministry, **grace empowerment** and **assignment**.

Grace is more than just God's attitude of favor towards us. It is the very substance of what enables us to live for Him and serve Him. "Grace empowerment" is the combination of natural ability, personality and spiritual gifting that the Lord sovereignly brings together within a person to enable us to make the contribution He desires us to make to His Kingdom economy. All that we are, all that we have, comes to us as a gift from His hand, by grace. Our calling, our ability, the particular gifts of the Holy Spirit we may function in and any servant-leadership role we may play, all come as a gift. we did not earn them. It is His grace that empowers us to serve Him. As Paul said in defending his apostleship - *"I am what I am by the grace of God."* (1 Corinthians 15:10)

While the implantation and impartation of this grace within us and to us comes from the sovereign hand of God alone, it comes through the agency of His community. Again, even as Paul had a sovereign, personal encounter with Jesus on the Damascus Road (Acts 9), Jesus immediately directs him to Ananias and the Church in Damascus. The call for Paul to be the Lord's "chosen instrument" was a sovereign act of God (Acts 6:15), but the facilitation of it came through the Lord's people: Ananias, then the disciples in Damascus, and then Barnabas.

Grace empowerment provides the ability to undertake your God-given assignment. To plant a church, he must empower you to do so. This is the role or place in the Body that God has for each of us - our function in the family business.

Paul was an Apostle to the Gentiles, Peter an Apostle to the Jews. Someone may have the grace empowerment that makes them a great Sunday School teacher or cell group leader, someone else may be designed by God to take food to the poor. Such assignments differ from person to person, yet one thing is common - one should serve only in an assignment for which they have a grace empowerment and for which they have the capacity of heart and character to sustain.

In Acts 13:1-3, the leaders of the Church in Antioch discerned that the will of the Lord was for Paul and Barnabas to be sent out on a missionary journey. Please note that those being sent were part of the discernment and decision making process, but were not the sole discerners or sole deciders. The leadership team of the Antioch community was instructed to set them apart (recognize or affirm) for the work the Lord had appointed them to do (ministry assignment). How different from our culture, where we as individuals decide what job we want to pursue, where we want to live, etc. This has been translated into the Church in our culture as well, as individual will and desire in ministry service is most often the determining factor in if and how we will serve. This is the opposite of submitting to the collective wisdom of community elders, who are charged, and burdened, with concern for the spiritual health and growth of the larger community. We recognize there have been abuses in this community of elders approach, as observed by many in the shepherding movements of the late seventies and eighties. The abuse does not negate the truth of this process. It only highlights the sad reality of our fallen nature.

In fact, Paul and Barnabas had only one relational crisis recorded in scripture - over John Mark. Acts 15:36-41 shows us how they disagreed over inclusion of John Mark on a mission trip from Antioch. Paul questions his capacity - *character/heart*, to undertake the trip - *the ministry assignment*.

The missionary church planting assignment of Barnabas and Paul was uncovered as the will of God in the context of life in community. Can the same be said of you? Can anyone else validate this calling you feel? Do your gifts and abilities match up with the role of church planter? How can you tell if this ministry assignment is from the Lord, or from your own heart. Your answers to these questions will say a lot about who you are, and how you are approaching your church plant. Knowing who you are in Christ, and what you are called to in Christ is essential to becoming a successful, fruitful church planter.

Your Personal Values

Everyone has things they value as being important. Whether by intention or not, we all have core values at the heart of who we are. Were someone to look at your calendar and checkbook, they could fairly quickly know the things that are important to you. Values are something that everyone possesses. Your behaviors indicate what your values are. Our **actual values** are those things we hold near and dear to our hearts, and indicated by patterns of regular and consistent behavior in various areas of our lives. We might say we value something, but unless we can point to specific, passionate behaviors in our life, then what we say is just a **preferred value**. This is something we'd like to do or be, but it is not really supported by our actions. If someone said they valued the Scripture, but then never read the bible, this would a preferred value. If they actually read the Bible on a regular, consistent basis, then it would be an actual value. Our values are what drive us; they define us, by governing our actions and reactions. Values say who you are.

Values are constant. Consequently, they rarely change. Your understanding of your values may expand and your thinking around them can become more focused. Values are passionate, as they generate passionate emotions and provide energy. Values are based on a Biblical world view that submits to the authority of the Lordship of Jesus Christ. They are our core convictions, as they influence everything we do. Our values have great influence on our attitudes, which then affect our behavior, which in turn validates our value system. What you really want in life or out of life is what will actually affect your behavior.

Understanding our personal values allows us to be in alignment with our own heart - our behavior coming from our convictions. To do something one does not agree with internally causes a discordant harmonic to set up within us: we are conflicted. Allowing our values to be our internal navigation system keeps our behavior in line with who we are. Paul talked about his own internal values conflict (Romans 7:21-25), how his behavior did not line up with his heart. So, it will be with all of us to some degree. However, Paul also gives us the answer: victory over this confliction comes through Jesus Christ. If our values are rooted in the Person of Christ, and we allow His Spirit to empower us to walk in Him daily, we can, with ever increasing consistency, see our behaviors driven by our values. For help in discovering your personal values, see Appendix 1.

Chapter Two R.E.A.D. Questions - "Who Are You?"

R -

- Based on your *reflection*, list the three major things that the Holy Spirit spoke to your heart regarding who you are in identity, capacity and destiny.
- *Reflect* on who has most impacted your life in a positive way and who has in a negative way.
- Take a moment and *reflect* on any "aha" moments you had while reading this chapter.

E -

- Based on the new awareness that you have gained, how would you *evaluate* your current life and church plant?
- *Evaluate* your church plant in light of who you are, your personal life sphere.
- *Evaluate* your church plant in light of your values: apply the T.E.R.M. test.

A -

What do you need to *adjust* on each of the above?

D -

What <u>will</u> you *do* about it?

CHAPTER 3 - WHAT DO YOU HAVE TO SAY?

You work so hard at it. Just remember that the rose never invites anyone to smell it. If it is fragrant, people will walk across the garden and endure the thorns to smell it. (Mahatma Gandhi)

When Tom was about to be sent out to plant his first church, at the ripe age of 29, one of the leaders in the church asked him a few questions:

"So, you want to start a new church?"

"Yes, that's right." Tom replied.

"You want to preach the Gospel?"

"Absolutely." Tom said.

"Well, what do you have to say?"

"What?"

"What do you have to say? Why should anyone listen to you?"

Taken quite off-guard by his friend's comments, it took Tom a moment to think through the question. No one had ever asked him what he would say when he preached, or why for that matter, why anyone should listen to him when he did. Tom soon realized the point his friend was making, the lesson he wanted Tom to learn.

Tom then answered this leader's questions by sharing what God had done in his life, and how these formative elements, these points of understanding and aspect of personal transformation combined to give him his message. The message he would preach would come from his own life, a unique message that came from his own walk with Christ, from the ways the Jesus' love had touched him, how His grace had changed him.

> *Praise be to the God and Father of our Lord Jesus Christ, the Father of compassion and the God of all comfort, who comforts us in all our troubles, so that we can comfort those in any trouble with the comfort we ourselves have received from God. For just as the sufferings of Christ flow over into our lives, so also through Christ our comfort overflows. If we are distressed, it is for your comfort and salvation; if we are comforted, it is for your comfort, which produces in you patient endurance of the same sufferings we suffer. And our hope for you is firm, because we know that just as you share in our sufferings, so also you share in our comfort. (2 Corinthians 1:3-7 ESV)*

We minister out of the comfort we have already received in Christ. In the last section we discussed knowing our identity in Christ, and how that shapes our life and ministry. now we wish to discuss how what we have experienced in God's grace forms the message of our life, and the corresponding ministry we have with others.

Comfort Received, Comfort Given

The apostle lays out the foundation of our ministries as he so wonderfully instructs that we can only give away what we have experienced ourselves. Ministry then flows from our being, who we are, allowing us to fulfill our God-given destiny. We can only give away what we have. All too often pastors do not give from who they are but who they believe they are supposed to be, a shadow self that lives in the world of external activities and duties, hoping to find inner fulfillment.

A Star Trek Voyager episode paints a wonderful picture of how the enemy taunts us and seeks to destroy us. In the episode, the emergency holographic doctor, who is an image produced by the computer through lasers that record on a photographic plate a diffraction pattern from which a three-dimensional image can be projected, is on the holodeck engaged in a program when the ship comes upon a mild disturbance that results in an electrical surge to the main computer system. The holodeck computer is affected and the doctor's program is altered. In the altered program, the doctor is portrayed as human, the rest of the ship as holograms, and the ship is in danger of being destroyed. In the program, a Starfleet officer comes on the scene and explains to the doctor that he is not a hologram, but the real doctor who created the program. He is actually at Starfleet in a simulation program of the Voyager that he created. Everything in the altered program indicated the Starfleet officer was telling the truth. The solution was to destroy the ship in the simulation and thus release the confused doctor and bring him back to reality. Just before he was to do it, a member of the real Voyager was projected in to the program to tell the holographic doctor to not destroy the ship. If he did so, he would end his program and destroy himself forever. Both sides were telling him that he would die if he acted wrongly. What was he to do? He was once sure of himself, but now he was not.

Like the doctor we often act in such ways that end up destroying or at least minimizing the self, and, instead of ministry flowing from our lives it tends to flow from our activities which deplete and drain our souls.

Mike is an Asian-American who was born in Pusan, Korea. Since he can recall he has struggled with the sting of being different, a foreigner if you will. Growing up as a child the idea of being a foreigner was not as well accepted as it is today, and Mike struggled with being different, both in America and in his homeland, Korea. Since he was mixed, he did not really fit in either country which marked and scarred his identity. To top that off, his dad, an American of English descent, said to Mike who was around eight years at the time: "You are a pretty good looking boy, now if you had your eyes operated on and made round like an American's you'd be a great looking boy." Not being good enough impacted Mike deeply and set in a motion a life of performance, and unknowingly, being a champion of the broken, downtrodden and rejected.

Struggling to be accepted, normal (whatever that is) was Mike's quest, to fit in by being better than others, being recognized through his accomplishments, etc, all of it to no avail since he could never shake off his looks.

Planting his first church at the age of 27 in Southern California was an exercise of passion for the lost and insecure, Mike, trying to be the pastor he thought everyone wanted. Ministering from outside of himself and not from who he was led Mike down a path of radical burnout and by the time he was 31 years old, with his church doing quite well, he found himself depressed, struggling with suicide, feeling unappreciated, bitter, and just extremely tired.

It's hard to give away comfort when you yourself have not received any in a long time. Dear church planter, whatever you do in this church plant, do it from the life you have experienced in God, the comfort you have found in Him, and the Jesus that you know. The trap of your church plant will be to plant the church you think everyone wants, the church you think is cool and effective, the church being everything but what God has done in you. No wonder so many pastors, after three to five years at their churches, find them to be places that do not resemble their heart and values.

The blind man who was healed by Jesus in John chapter 9 is the basis by which ever pastor and leader should operate. The blind man is questioned by the religious leaders who are arguing over whether Jesus was from God or not. and oddly enough miss the miraculous healing to focus on the violation of the Sabbath by Jesus. The man's parents are even questioned, but fearfully defer to their son to answer the question about the healing and Jesus. The former blind man responds to whether Jesus is a sinner or not, from God or not, with a very simple and profound response: "I don't know whether he is a sinner," the man replied. "But I know this: I was blind, and now I can see!" (John 9:25, NLT)

If we are going to plant churches from the comfort we have

received, then we have to share the Jesus that we know. The blind man did not know all about Jesus, he simply knew he was blind and now he could see. Later in the passage Jesus finds the man and reveals to him who he truly is. No matter how you slice the story, the blind man would always know Jesus as the one who healed him. Maybe that is what it means to share from the comfort you have received, giving away the Jesus that you know. Not the Jesus that Rick Warren knows or the one that Bill Hybels knows; nor a Jesus that you have simply read about, systematized and categorized but a Jesus that you have encountered, continue to encounter and know from a life experience. As Mike often says, "I know Jesus is doing fine today because I just had breakfast with Him."

Your church plant will be based around your life story, the comfort you have received, which will be the driving thrust to what you have to say, your life message. It is rather ironic that of the three items that bring victory for the faithful listed by John in the book of Revelation, we find one that seems almost out of place. John writes: "And they have defeated him because of the blood of the Lamb and because of their testimony. And they were not afraid to die." (Revelation 12:11, NLT) There it sits, loud and clear, church planter, one of the keys to overcoming the enemy of our souls is your "testimony" – your story, sharing the Jesus that you know, passing on the comfort that you have received. No one is more qualified than you to do so and whatever the enemy brings your way to discourage you he can never take away the Jesus that you know. You may not know all the answers to life, be able to answer everyone's questions about tragedies, catastrophes, the will of God, and human inequity, but you can answer the question of who you know Jesus to be in your life. "I don't know whether he is a sinner," the man replied. "But I know this: I was blind, and now I can see!" Base your church plant on what you are most certain of in your life, and let your church be built upon that comfort you have received as you incarnate your life message before the people God has called you to.

God's Unique Design

As we have seen, every person is a unique work of art from the hands of the magnificent potter Himself. There is no question that God uniquely shapes each Christian with giftings, talents, personality and ability to fulfill all that He has so wonderfully designed for him/her. With that said, is it possible that the question of "Who am I?" is best answered by discovering the "why" first? If it is true that the "nature of a thing is defined by the purpose of a thing," then it would only seem right to ask the question of "Why am I?" To grasp why the Father has made us is then the key to understanding our lives and ministries.

To grasp the truth that the creator of all things has so intimately and intricately shaped you is a reality that many of the faith have not come to understand. For any ministry to experience the fullness God has designed, it is necessary that the leader come to understand how the hand of God has shaped his/her life for this appointed season and task. When we discover the sovereign nature of God's design in our lives, it becomes clear that our lives and ministries contribute to establishing the reign of God in our land.

> *Story is the primary way in which revelation of God is given to us. The Holy Spirit's literary genre of choice is story. Story isn't a simple or a naïve form of speech from which we graduate to the more sophisticated, 'higher' languages of philosophy or mathematics, leaving the stories behind for children and the less educated. From beginning to end, our Scriptures are primarily written in the form of story. The biblical story comprises other literary forms—sermons and genealogies, prayers and letter, poems and proverbs—but story carries them all in its capacious and organically intricate plot. Moses told stories; Jesus told stories; the four Gospel writers presented their good news in the form of stories. And the Holy Spirit weaves all this*

storytelling into the vast and holy literary architecture that reveals God to us as Father, Son, and Holy Spirit in the way that he chooses to make himself known. Story. To get this revelation right, we enter the story . . . God reveals himself to us not in a metaphysical formulation or a cosmic fireworks display but in the kind of stories that we use to tell our children who they are and how to grow up as human beings, tell our friends who we are and what it's like to be human. Story is the most adequate way we have of accounting for our lives, noticing the obscure details that turn out to be pivotal, appreciating the subtle accents of color and form and scent that give texture to our actions and feelings, giving coherence to our meeting and relationships in work and family, finding our precise place in the neighborhood and in history . . . Story is the primary means we have for learning what the world is, and what it means to be a human being in it. (Eugene Peterson, Leap Over a Wall, p.p. 3-4)

What is critical to understand as a leader is that our lives are more than our ministries. We need to have a developing picture of who we are and how our unique giftedness will be utilized in our ministry. The ministry does not define us. Rather, it is an expression of who we are. We are individuals first who are called to this wonderful enterprise of ministry. Exploring how God has shaped us for this season is an important step to serving the Lord in our unique capacities. We each are story being written by God, individual stories that comprise a larger story which we might call His-story. We have been called to partner with the divine author as he pens His-story in our lives, manifesting and incarnating Jesus through each of us.

As noted earlier, the unique aspect to our lives is often ignored and even rejected. Mike spent 35 years of his life trying not to be Asian only to be reminded every time he looked in the mirror that he was. It was not until he was in his late 30's that he began to embrace his Asian, side (after all, his dad didn't think it valuable, so why should he). Once he began to embrace it, something beautiful happened. Doors to ethnic ministry began to open up and Mike suddenly found himself pastoring a church that was comprised of Filipinos, Hispanics, Chinese, etc. Once he accepted his multi-faceted state of being an Asian-American, the universe of his ministry expanded beyond what he ever thought possible. Ministry has (at this time of writing) expanded to included some form of ministry and even churches in Africa, Philippines, Fiji, Baja Mexico, Vietnam, India, Russia, Ireland, Dominican Republic, and China.

Church planter, embrace you who you are! Accept what Jesus has done and is doing in your life, live out and share the Jesus you know, and watch God do marvelous exploits through your life as you pass on the greatest news our universe has ever known: The Creator loves them, knows them, and wants to spend an eternity with them.

Chapter Three R.E.A.D. Questions - "What Do You Have To Say?"

R -

- Based on your *reflection*, list the three major things that the Holy Spirit spoke to your heart regarding your life message.
- *Reflect* on the Jesus that you know – who is He and what He has done in your life?
- What are the passion points in your life? What ignites your heart? What breaks it?
- If you didn't have to worry about failure, how would you live your life? How would you do ministry?

E -

- Based on the new awareness that you have gained, how would you *evaluate* your current life and church plant in relationship to the Jesus that you know?
- *Evaluate* how you are sharing and living out the comfort you have received?
- *Evaluate* how your church plant will help people find their life message?

A -

What do you need to *adjust* on each of the above?

D -

What <u>will</u> you *do* about it?

CHAPTER 4 - ARE YOU READY?

God prepares us throughout our life to serve Him. This is true for everyone in the body of Christ. He develops us in both our character and our abilities. Throughout the Bible we see person after person going through seasons of preparation prior to release to the role through which they make their ultimate contribution. For those called to serve Him in pastoral ministry, these times of preparation come before God moves us into the next assignment we have. They prepare us spiritual, practically and experientially, so that our service might make the most fruitful contribution to the Kingdom economy possible. As part of that preparation, He allows us to be tested, indeed, even tempted. The Wilderness Temptation of Christ is a good example of this, as Jesus Himself was tested as the culmination of His preparation before starting His public ministry. In the post-Christian West, people are looking for something authentic. Your preparation for the ministry of church planting is essential in God's formative process as he shapes you into an authentic son or daughter of God.

The Passing Big Three

There are three tests which God allows that are common among church planters, three aspects of our life and character that he validates before releasing us to our assignment. By allowing a test of our **stewardship**, the Lord validates both our heart towards Him and our abilities in the area of resource management. In testing our **submission to authority**, the Lord prepares us to function in dependency on Him, and to serve as a representative authority for Him. Through the **test of endurance** He builds our stamina, steadfastness and faith. Let's examine each of these in depth.

The Test of Stewardship

Being a steward entails caring for something that is not our own as if it were. Stewardship, or having a place of responsibility for caring for or cultivating someone or something, is a key Principle in the Kingdom of God. All that we have, all that we are or ever will be comes from Him. Our very life is not our own, but belongs to the Creator who made us. Our spouse, our family, our money are not really our possessions; they are merely entrusted to our care as His stewards.

The Stewardship of Life

Since organic life flows from the inside out, the life of a pastor should operate in the same fashion which is precisely what Paul implied in giving away the comfort we have received. We can give away what we possess or, better said, what possesses us. In the first test we are asked to be stewards of our life. If health is to flow from the life of the church, then it must be infused by the life of the leader and the leadership community. Christianity is not simply a religion of do's and don'ts. It is a way of life. Our Westernized way of doing church helps people know how to do church for two hours every week, but it does not model for them how to live out the Christian faith as a human being.

Church planter, whatever you do you must learn to provide self care because no one else will. Just in case you are thinking that we are advocating a life selfishness, let us remind you that **Jesus died for the church and so you don't have to**. You get to live for the church and incarnate the gospel to a world that needs hope, and you'll do your best if you practice the rhythms of grace that God set in motion. Keep in mind that being busy is not the mark of an effective pastor. Eugene Peterson writes: "The adjective *busy* set as a modifier to *pastor* should sound to our ears like *adulterous* to characterize a wife or *embezzling* to describe a banker. It is an outrageous scandal, a blasphemous affront." The life of a pastor is not meant to be a life of simply being busy but one that is holy, free, set apart for the God's glory and joy, full of life and the fruit that bears more life. Being busy does not mean you are effective (it can make you less effective), instead being effective makes you effective. From a boxing perspective, throwing lots of punches does not make you a good fighter, just a tired one. Throwing the right and most effective punches is what makes you a good and effective fighter.

The first place, dear church planter, that you are called to model your faith and share your love and life is in your home. Whatever you are, you are first God's son/daughter, then a spouse, a parent and finally a called son/daughter for the purpose of the Kingdom of God. Don't sacrifice your family for the sake of the Gospel. Instead love them and nurture them for the sake of the Gospel and model to your church what it means to be a son/daughter of the King in real life, not just in church for two hours per week. As a matter of fact, how your relational life is at home will eventually be reflected in your staff relations and church relations. For example, if your spouse feels neglected and unimportant because of your workaholic tendencies, then over the course of three to five years your staff and even church will begin to feel the same. Whatever health or unhealth we have in our interior worlds will spill over into all of our relationships, and that particular DNA strand will multiply.

Mike has two daughters and one day his oldest daughter (age five at the time of writing) playfully called him "Pastor Mike." She did this because all the people in church call him that and it was an endearing and playful moment. Mike knelt down and smiled and gently said, "I am Pastor Mike to all the people in the church but I am your daddy and will always be your daddy first." Whatever we are in life and however effective our ministries, may they never be marked with failure at home because we are overly consumed with the "out there," and forget what was "in here" at our homes. Remember, if you tend to neglect those closest to you, it won't be long before the staff and church people become those closest to you and guess what, the cycle starts all over again. Just be careful!

We'd like to list some key rhythms for you to incorporate into your life.

First, have daily encounters with God: through prayer and reflective reading of the Word. Such meditation anchors oneself in the morning and de-fragments the mental hard drive at night by reflecting over the day and what God has done and spoken to you through the day.

Second, establish a Sabbath rhythm: God rested one day a week, and it would be right and good for us to do the same. Find a day where you cease the activity of the ministry, and simply enjoy life with God, your family, your children.

Next establish reflective rhythms: Wisdom only comes by way of reflection. That is reflecting on one's life and happenings. All the knowledge in the world will not help you know what to do. It is wisdom that helps us navigate the complicated seas of life knowing. Being knowledgeable and being wise is not necessarily the same thing. Be sure to establish monthly and annual rhythms for yourself. For example, take time to read and nourish your soul weekly (at least monthly). Find time to reflect each week on what God is saying and doing in your life, plan days in the month where you do nothing but read and pray and seek God, and plan at least two days per year where you spend time with God listening, reflecting and assessing yourself, the church, ministry, the vision, etc.

Proper rest: David says "Unless the Lord builds a house, the work of the builders is useless. Unless the Lord protects a city, guarding it with sentries will do no good. It is useless for you to work so hard from early morning until late at night, anxiously working for food to eat; for God gives rest to his loved ones." (Psalm 127:1-2, NLT) We need to allow ourselves to trust God by resting. Dr. Archibald Hart would encourage us to sleep nine hours a day. Whether you can rest that many hours per day or not, it is important that we rest a proper amount every night. We recommend that you take some time and read through Dr. Hart's book, *The Hidden Link Between Adrenaline and Stress*.

Monthly date night: With all the demands of ministry we recommend at least a monthly date night (weekly preferred) where the husband and wife go out without the kids and just enjoy each other, talk, share, watch a good movie, eat, etc. The only way to keep the romantic fires of marriage going is by being together and intentionally fanning the flames of love. Be the example to your congregation of a godly spouse who is caring, loving – you know, like Jesus.

Family Night: We believe this should be weekly where there is a night solely dedicated to the family where you enjoy each other by playing games, going to movies, watching movies at home, going on hikes, etc. This is particularly vital when your kids are under 13 years of age, as the vital aspects of personality and values are set within that time frame.

Here are a few more practical suggestions for you to consider. We'd like to recommend that you tell your spouse daily at least one thing you appreciate about them, tell your children regularly about your love for them, tell them you are "proud of them" as you model the love of God for them. Incorporate your children into the spiritual realities of Christianity as a family, not as a pastor. Our children should learn to pray not only because we have taught them, but because we pray. Every opportunity in life is an opportunity to teach your children the way of Jesus. There was a baby dedication Mike was asked to do in the home of a Filipino family. The house was packed with family and friends. Mike's oldest daughter, Sierra (age five at the time) was keenly watching. Mike leaned down and asked Sierra if she would like to help daddy and of course she said yes. Mike then told her that he was going to put some oil on her finger and he would like her to place it on the baby's head and then ask Jesus to bless the little baby. Sierra took the anointing oil and, like she was standing before the Holy of Holies, touched the forehead of the little boy and asked Jesus to bless the little baby. It was not a practiced moment, but one that flowed from the life of a family that looks for every opportunity to be followers of Christ in real life affairs, not just ministry appointed times.

The Stewardship of Finances

It is truly amazing how much the New Testament talks about money. The New Testament says the love of it is the root of all kinds of evil (1 Timothy 6:10), that you can't serve it and God (Luke 16:13), and in Ecclesiastes that if you love money, you will never feel like you have enough (Ecclesiastes 5:10). The one passage that really catches our eye is Luke 16:10-13:

> *One who is faithful in a very little is also faithful in much, and one who is dishonest in a very little is also dishonest in much. If then you have not been faithful in the unrighteous wealth, who will entrust to you the true riches? And if you have not been faithful in that which is another's, who will give you that which is your own? No servant can serve two masters, for either he will hate the one and love the other, or he will be devoted to the one and despise the other. You cannot serve God and money.*

Here Jesus is contrasting the relative worthlessness of the common currency and the true riches of the Kingdom of God, but, He indicates that both our heart attitude towards money and how we handle it are indicative of our trustworthiness in dealing with the true riches of the Kingdom. He wants to co-labor with you in the harvest field of the city or town you are going into, and He likes to know how His partners will perform.

A senior leader in a local church must be free from the love of money (1 Timothy 3:3), and let's get this straight, if you are church planting, there probably isn't going to be a ton of money involved, either in personal income or in resources for the church. On the practical level, management of personal funds is a good benchmark of how you will manage church funds. Learning to discipline yourself in the use of money in your personal affairs will transfer into good management of ministry funds. (Setting up good financial practices and systems is essential from day one of a church plant.) The bigger picture here is about the heart: Can God trust with the things of the Kingdom if he can't trust you with a few bucks? He will be using you to influence the destiny of souls. He needs to verify your character.

So, what can you do to pass the test of finances? Here are a few thoughts in proving your faithfulness in this area:

First of all, tithe. If you haven't developed this discipline yet, better start now. Tithing has been given to us as a means of reminding us of our dependency on God, the source of our life and provision (Malachi 3:8-10). As a church planter, starting from scratch in your new work, you will be completely dependent on His grace for everything. Start now. Don't wait, don't rationalize: Take ten percent off the top and give to the Lord.

Set a personal budget and live within your means. Now you have 90 percent left to pay your taxes and live on. If you have any credit debt, loans, payments, etc., do your best to eliminate them. Get rid of your credit cards, use a debit card or a charge card on which you must pay off the balance monthly. Most Christian financial counselors would tell you that the only debt payment that you should carry is a mortgage, as the property is an investment and will appreciate. Be wise about your choice of home or housing situations. Don't get in over your head. It also makes sense to wait until you are sure of the target location before settling into a home.

Pay your bills on time. In 1 Timothy 3, one of the qualifications for being an Elder relates to respect in the community: *Moreover, he must be well thought of by outsiders, so that he may not fall into disgrace, into a snare of the devil. (1 Timothy 3:7)* Failure to pay one's bills on time can have a serious impact on your witness, reflecting poorly on the Lord and the ministry of the church. The same is true of taxes: pay what is due by law. Be above board on everything (Romans 13:6-8).

Be prepared to work a job while planting. We believe that a *first-time* church planter should work a secular job or at least find support outside the church until the church reaches 75-90 people. Up to that point the monies are better spent investing into the ministry of the church. This is not to say the church planter should not be compensated, but to reinforce the reality that a church planter does far better finding ways to connect with the community, and a job is a great way to do just that. Having a job also limits the time of the church planter which encourages involvement from others, putting the church planter in a position of developing people for Christ and helping them find their God-given destinies. More simply, people won't expect you to do it all because you can't. On top of that with a congregation of 50 or so people, a full-time pastor would have too much time on his hands to over-prepare a message, could even visit everyone with time left over. This could all result in a rather non-missional foundation.

The Stewardship of Ministry

Another aspect of the stewardship test is the faithful completion of ministry and ministry commitments prior to the Lord releasing you to your plant. He who is faithful in little will be faithful in much (Luke 16:10). Before you can take on more Kingdom responsibility, you must be proven as being faithful in what has already been released to you. This touches on both character capacity and ministry competencies. While you are filled with vision for the future, how are you serving the leaders and people where the Lord has placed you now? Are you ending your current assignments well, or leaving others in the lurch? Concerning competencies – your calling and vision to plant cannot be a substitute for your being developed in your ministry skills. Calling and ability are two different things. Your stewardship of your current ministry is the way the Lord prepares your skill set for future ministry.

The Test of Submission

King David was an incredible guy. As a young man he was chosen by God to replace Saul as King of Israel. Anointed by the prophet Samuel long before Saul's reign was over, David lived in the tension of being called by the Lord to serve His people in a place of authority, but without the release to pursue that destiny. As long as Saul was king, David could not be, and furthermore he had to submit to Saul as the God-appointed King over Israel until such time as God removed him. Now, this would be hard for any young man to put up with, but the situation was compounded by the problem that Saul at times was quite mad. In fact, it seems as if he was in some way afflicted with a demonic spirit. Not just your everyday, run-of-the-mill demonic spirit, but one that drove him to such paranoia concerning David that Saul repeatedly tried to kill him. David spent a good deal of time during this period of his life ducking the spears Saul was tossing and hiding out in caves. But he never struck back at Saul. He just ducked and ran for cover. Why didn't he fight back? There were several times when he could have killed Saul, but chose not to. Why? Because David knew he could not raise his hand against the Lord's anointed (1 Samuel 24:6). What? Saul was a wacko, with a demon on board as well! But he was still the Lord's chosen one, the anointed, and was king of Israel until the Lord removed him. As such, David could not attack him or usurp the throne by violence. Saul was a flawed and fallen leader who David had to submit to, even though Saul was misusing the authority he had. David submitted in that he would not strike the Lord's anointed. He submitted to the Lord by recognizing His choice of Saul as king. He did not submit to Saul's broken humanity. He did not allow himself to be abused or be killed: He ducked and ran, but he never shot back.

Saul was a classic example of what you might call "bad authority." Every church planter, indeed, every emerging church leader will face a test from the Lord before being released into a new place of Kingdom responsibility. That test will involve submitting to an authority that may not understand you or know you, someone who may have expectations of you which seem unreasonable. It may involve jumping through hoops you don't see the need for. Whatever it is, however it comes, you will be tested, just like David. Hopefully, this leader or authority won't be trying to stick you with a spear. And more likely than not, it probably won't require you to live in a cave in the desert with a bunch of debtors and brigands.

This test is as much about you learning how to be in a place of authority as it is to be under authority. God never releases us to be in authority unless we are under authority, and never until we can rightly be trusted to not be bad authority ourselves. We might release ourselves, but He won't. The authority we are talking about has skin on: It is incarnated in a person. We can't just say, "Well, I'm submitted to the Lord, not man." Guess what: If you're not submitted to the Lord's authority that He has invested in a person, you are not submitted to the Lord. We are called to obey those over us in the Lord, not as robots or as slaves, but with the proper heart reverencing their position of responsibility before the Lord.

> *Obey your leaders and submit to them, for they are keeping watch over your souls, as those who will have to give an account. Let them do this with joy and not with groaning, for that would be of no advantage to you. (Hebrews 13:17)*

Remember, this is a test! How you respond to it determines the future outcomes of your life and ministry. What you sow into the life and ministry of another person who may be a leader to you in the Lord, perhaps a pastor, a mentor, a denominational overseer, that is what you will reap in your own life and ministry. Does this seem too cause and effect for you? Paul seems to think that was the way it works: *Do not be deceived: God is not mocked, for whatever one sows, that will he also reap. For the one who sows to his own flesh will from the flesh reap corruption, but the one who sows to the Spirit will from the Spirit reap eternal life.(Galatians 6:7-8)*

Respond to bad authority, even if you are hurt or wronged, at the impulse of your flesh, and you will reap the same response in the future from someone else. Respond in the Spirit of God by giving grace and by submission, and you too will be the recipient of grace, honor and deference in those you lead. Whatever was lacking in the "bad authority" is an opportunity to develop that godly trait in you. In other words, whatever was lacking in the life of the leader is what you get to become. Rather than focusing or reacting to the hurt, forgive it and become the person that leader was not to you so that others might benefit from the Jesus in you.

The Test of Endurance

Church planting is not a sprint, it's a marathon. Endurance is key, as the Lord indicated to Jeremiah –

If you have raced with men on foot, and they have wearied you, how will you compete with horses? And if in a safe land you are so trusting, what will you do in the thicket of the Jordan? (Jeremiah 12:5)

Prior to beginning your church planting project, the Lord will allow you to be placed in situations that build your spiritual and emotional endurance. You will be stretched, and it may not be easy. However, much of your fruitfulness in planting will be around the issue of simply outlasting the Enemy of your soul. You will face life, ministry and potential job transitions in the first phase of your plant, as you reorient yourself to align with this new chapter of service the Lord is bringing you into. Initial results in your ministry efforts may not prove fruitful. Most planters underestimate the amount of time needed to get a new church rolling. Persistence and perseverance will be required to push through. Church planting will quite probably be the most difficult thing you ever do in life. In all this, the Lord is able to make you stand (Romans 14:4) if you simply don't loose heart (Ephesians 6:11-13).

While you can never be completely ready to plant a church, you can participate with the Lord in His preparation, recognizing His hand in your life, shaping you and forming you in preparation for making your contribution to His Kingdom. You will always be dependant on Him, and yet, you do not want to cut short His preparatory work in your life.

Chapter Four R.E.A.D. Questions - "Are You Ready?"

R -

- Based on your *reflection*, list the three major things that the Holy Spirit spoke to your heart regarding the test of stewardship, submission and endurance.
- *Reflect* on your current process of self care.
- *Reflect* on how you require submission of your leaders.
- *Reflect* on what you could do less of and what you could do more of. In other words are you doing what matters over what is just sometimes "busy" work.

E -

- Based on the new awareness that you have gained, how would you *evaluate* your current life and church plant in relationship to the tests of stewardship, submission and endurance?
- *Evaluate* how your life reflects the same submission process you require of your leaders.
- *Evaluate* how your church plant will help people live the way of Christianity instead of just doing church.

A -

What do you need to *adjust* on each of the above?

D -

What <u>will</u> you *do* about it?

CHAPTER 5 - WHAT IS YOUR QUEST?

A water bearer in India had two large pots. Each hung on opposite ends of a pole that the bearer carried across his neck. One of the pots had a crack in it, while the other was perfect. The latter always delivered a full portion of water at the end of the long walk from the stream to the master's house. The cracked pot arrived only half-full. Everyday for a full two years, the water-bearer delivered only one and a half pots of water.

The perfect pot was proud of its accomplishments, because it fulfilled magnificently the purpose for which it had been made. But the poor cracked pot was ashamed of its imperfections, miserable that it was able to accomplish only half of what it had been made to do. After the second year of what it perceived to be a bitter failure, the unhappy pot spoke to the water-bearer one day by the stream.

"I am ashamed of myself, and I want to apologize to you," the pot said.

"Why?" asked the bearer. "What are you ashamed of?"

"I have been able, for these past two years, to deliver only half my load, because this crack in my side causes water to leak out all the way back to your master's house. Because of my flaws, you have to do all this work, and you don't get full value from your efforts," the pot said.

The water-bearer felt sorry for the old cracked pot, and in his compassion, he said, "As we return to the master's house, I want you to notice the beautiful flowers along the path." Indeed, as they went up the hill, the cracked pot took notice of the beautiful wildflowers on the side of the path, bright in the sun's glow, and the sight cheered it up a bit.

But at the end of the trail, it still felt badly because it had leaked out half its load, and so again it apologized to the bearer for its failure.

The bearer said to the pot, "Did you notice that there were flowers only on your side of the path, not on the other pot's side? That is because I have always known about your flaw, and I have taken advantage of it. I planted flower seeds on your side of the path, and everyday, as we have walked back from the stream, you have watered them. For two years I have been able to pick these beautiful flowers to decorate my master's table. Without you being just the way you are, he would not have had this beauty to grace his house.

The moral of the story can easily be surmised in the following. Being a cracked pot is a good thing, and we should allow Jesus to use our cracks and flaws to grace his Father's table. Our vision quest is not based on some model of perfection that we are called to live, but a real life faith that is expressed in the humble cloth of human imperfection. Like the cracked pot who was stunned by the water-bearer's words, "Without you being just the way you are, the master would not have had this beauty to grace his house." The pot had assumed that the sole purpose of its existence was to haul water from the stream to the house. Enfolded within its narrow self-determination, the flawed pot had not suspected God's grand purpose for it: to give life to the dormant flower seeds along the path. Within your vision quest, realize that God has a grand purpose for you that will, oddly enough, flow from the brokenness of your life to heal the brokenness of the people He has called you to.

Definition of Vision

100 years after the Emancipation Proclamation had been signed, and Martin Luther King, Jr. delivered an historic speech at

the Lincoln Memorial on August 18, 1963 that cast his vision for the America he had lived and eventually died for. In that historic speech Dr. King said:

> *So I say to you, my friends, that even though we must face the difficulties of today and tomorrow, I still have a dream. It is a dream deeply rooted in the American dream that one day this nation will rise up and live out the true meaning of its creed—we hold these truths as self-evident, that all men are created equal.*
>
> *I have a dream that one day on the red hills of Georgia, sons of former slaves and sons of former slave-owners will be able to sit down together at the table of brotherhood.*
>
> *I have a dream that one day, even the state of Mississippi, a state sweltering with the heat of injustice, sweltering with the heat of oppression will be transformed into an oasis of freedom and justice.*
>
> *I have a dream that my four little children will one day live in a nation where they will not be judged by the color of their skin but by the content of their character. I have a dream today!*
>
> *I have a dream that one day, down in Alabama, with its vicious racists, with its governor having his lips dripping with the words of interposition and nullification, that one day right there in Alabama, little black boys and black girls will be able to join hands with little white boys and white girls as sisters and brothers.*
>
> *I have a dream that one day every valley shall be exalted, every hill and mountain shall be made low, the rough places will be made plain, and the crooked places will be made straight, and the glory of the Lord will be revealed, and all flesh shall see it together.*
>
> *This is our hope. This is the faith with which I return to the*

South with.

With this faith we will be able to hew out of the mountain of despair a stone of hope. With this faith we will be able to transform the jangling discords of our nation into a beautiful symphony of brotherhood. With this faith we will be able to work together, to pray together, to struggle together, to go to jail together, to stand up for freedom together, knowing that we will be free one day...

And when we allow freedom to ring, when we let it ring from every village and every hamlet, from every state and every city, we will be able to speed up that day when all of God's children, black men and white men, Jews and Gentiles, Protestants and Catholics, will be able to join hands and sing in the words of the old Negro spiritual, "Free at last, free at last; thank God Almighty, we are free at last." (Martin Luther King Jr. I Have A Dream: Writings and Speeches, ed. By James M. Washington, pp. 101-106)

Dr. King clearly captures our hearts and imaginations as he paints a picture of a future that we now live in, a future he did not get to see with his human eyes but saw with his eyes of faith and vision that ignited a nation and paved the way for where we are today. What is that dream in your heart that seeks to plant a church within the confines of a community, a city, and change the spiritual dynamics of the culture around you? What is that vision that has so captured your life that when you share it with others, they find their hearts stirring within and are compelled to see what you see?

Vision begins with a dream and defines the WHAT we are called to *become* and *do*. Vision is the purifying agent in our ministry process, keeping us on track and on course to what has God has called us to become and do. For Dr. King there were many issues of social injustice that could have sidetracked him but the vision. The dream he had kept him on course to see the future he was dreaming of become a reality in the now.

Vision is what burns in your heart about a preferred future that you give your life to, so that it might become a reality in the here and now. A clear characteristic about godly vision is that it will be something that you cannot possibly achieve by your own power and will. Achieving this God-given vision will need the concerted hearts and efforts from others, and a strong dependence upon the Holy Spirit.

However, one must keep in mind that unlike values, mission and purpose, the vision is dynamic and more subject to change. If the vision does undergo change, it does so only at the margins and not at its core. We do believe that God places the vision within a primary vision carrier, as evidenced all throughout scripture, but that God unpacks it through a leadership community. It could be said that God gives the vision in black and white to the vision carrier, and the leadership community provides the color and fullness to it.

Community Vision

There are few things we can about vision. Let us qualify our understanding here by making plain that vision is God's authority in the church. It allows leadership to say "yes" and "no" on ministry choices.

Vision is God's preferred future and involves both being and doing, not just being task oriented. Dr. King's speech did not contain any real action points, just a dream. Mission is best understood as how we will flesh out the vision, but we must note that vision is all inclusive and does involve both being and doing.

Vision in its truest sense is who we are we becoming and seeking to become. This might be the question of life: "Who are you becoming?" "What is your church becoming?"

Vision is what we want to see happen through the church community: That which is happening to the church community is then extended and given beyond the church community to the city. Again, from the comfort we have received we give.

Vision is what maturing into the fullness of Christ would look like for your congregation, and how that is manifested in the fruit of the Spirit, through godliness in relationships, in Missional fruitfulness, which includes the transformational component you desire to bring to the local social order, and what the impact on people will look like.

Vision Questioned and Applied

Practically, then vision will be able to answer these questions:
> What would you expect your church community to look like in three years?
>
> What would you expect your church community to look like in three years in relationship to character and being? In relationship to acts that describe your community (doing)?
>
> What would you expect your church community to look like in three years regarding maturity in behavior and ministry?
>
> What would you expect your church community to look like in three years in relationship to fruitfulness and social transformation?
>
> What metaphor do you employ to describe your dream?

Your vision is your target, the thing which you are aiming for, and the thing the Lord uses to focus our ministry towards His preferred future. This is your quest – the quest to realize the incarnation of Jesus in your new church community.

Chapter Five R.E.A.D. Questions - "What Is Your Quest?"

R -

- Based on your *reflection*, list the three major things that the Holy Spirit spoke to you about your vision quest.
- *Reflect* on your current process of casting vision.
- *Reflect* on how you share your vision with people.
- *Reflect* on your dream and share it utilizing Dr. King's language of "I have a dream," and go on to describe your dream.

E -

- Based on the new awareness that you have gained, how would you *evaluate* your current life and church plant in relationship to the vision you see?
- *Evaluate* how your life reflects and embodies the vision.
- *Evaluate* how your church plant will help people live out and become the vision.

A -

What do you need to *adjust* on each of the above?

D -

What <u>will</u> you *do* about it?

PART 2 – DNA TRANSMISSION & MULTIPLICATION

CHAPTER 6 – WHO IS YOUR COMMUNITY?

Jesus as The Source

In Christianity we look to Christ for the basis of our salvation, and rightfully so. We thought we'd go one step further and not only look to Jesus for our salvation, but as the basis of our life, ministry philosophy and practice.

We do not believe Jesus came to establish a religion but a revolution of heart, releasing the captive human heart by setting it free of the bondage of sin and brokenness, and restoring our fallen humanity to the original design and intent of our Creator. All that to say: Jesus came not only **as** a way for life for us spiritually (salvation), but to establish a way **of** life for us (daily practice).

This chapter will provide you with a basic philosophy of ministry, and with principles to guide your ministry taken straight from the life and ministry of Jesus. After all, our Savior was pretty good at raising up disciples, developing leaders and did start a movement. Let's take a look.

Together We Stand

Before we proceed, it would be important for us to note that the Bible makes it quite clear that the early church was unified in purpose and mission. They were together. Acts 1:14 tells us that **"They *all* met continually for prayer."** Luke tells us that the early church shared all things in common (Acts 2:43-47). In simple language, they lived together and served the Lord together. Even Peter's inaugural sermon that gave birth to the church was not a solitary act. Luke adds the rather stunning fact that in that momentous sermon at Pentecost, Peter preached with boldness and thousands came to receive Christ. We often have a picture of Peter preaching as a solitary act when it was a communal act, shared by the leadership community. Luke provides the clarifying line that **"Peter stepped forward with the eleven other apostles."** (Acts 2:14) This was not about a hero or some superstar that gave birth to the church, but about twelve men, a community, a fellowship who had given their lives to the person of Jesus, working together to declare the name that brings life to all who call upon Him. The early church was clearly a church in relationship with God and in relationship with each other. The basis of all church life is then in these two relationships.

Scripture makes it quite clear that the basis of all relationships is our relationship with God, which is reflected in one word: Love. The apostle John writes: *"Beloved, let us love one another; for love is of God, and he who loves is born of God and know God. He who does not love does not know God; for God is love."* (I John 4:7-8, NLT)

Relationship is vital to church life because we are the children of a God who is personal, creating us in such a way that reflects His very nature. To be created in the Image of God is to be fashioned in God likeness, as the passage in Genesis 1:26-27 suggests. If you will permit us to do a little philosophizing with you and walk you into the world of theology, we would like to show you how we understand relationship.

The Genesis account boldly asserts that we have been created in the "Image of God." To be fashioned in this way is to be in God likeness for the "likeness of God."

What Does it Mean to be in the Likeness of God?

One of the characteristics is found in the word, *"Us."* The point is communion within the Godhead is taking place. The Godhead is deliberating within itself regarding the creation of man. There is a Divine dialogue taking place. What we learn from this is three simple things: **God is relational; God is triune, yet one unity; God is love.**

God is a relational. Relationship, based in love, is at the very heart of God's nature. We are created to be in relationship with Him and the creation (Mark 12:29-31), to love God and our neighbor. Remember, it was God who said that it wasn't good for man to be alone. Relationship with God is primary and crucial for one's sense of self, as is relationship with others.

God is triune, yet one unity. As the body of Christ we are to be one as the Father and Son are one. John writes, "that they may be one even as we are one, I in them and thou in me, so that the world may know that thou hast sent me and hast loved them even as thou hast loved me" (John 17:22b-23), and "that they may be one, even as we are one" (17:11).

God is love. We love because God first loved us (I John 4:19). The heart of the Father is love, and love is a relational reality. Jonathan demonstrates love for us at the human level. Scripture says that he loved David as he loved himself (I Samuel 20:17).

As a church planter, you will want to address the issue of relationship and learn to be relational in all your endeavors, keeping in mind that we are human beings and not human doings. Relationship is the foundational fabric of the church and human life. In reality all problems and struggles that people have within churches (in life, family, politics as well) are more relational than theological. What you will want to find the answer for in this section is the question: "Who will you be together as a community of God's people?"

It is much easier to answer the question of "what would Jesus do?" than address the deeper reality of "who would be Jesus be?" in this situation. "Being" involves heart and the totality of the person whereas "doing" does not necessitate such. The question we are asking you to prayerfully ponder and answer is then twofold: "Who am I becoming?" and for the community "Who are we becoming?"

Core Community

Borrowing from the life and ministry of Jesus we see some key principles and steps that might be beneficial for our churches. Gathering and developing your core community is absolutely critical since the core community will live out your values, vision and mission. More simply put, your community will be a reflection of who you are, and who you are to them is what they will reproduce. This is the reality of DNA. Many church planters don't recognize their church plant after 3-5 years because there is a values clash. It starts with a planter who clashes with his/her own values, verbalizing one set of values while living another.

Let us summarize the highlights of Jesus' ministry. When Jesus began His public ministry He did the following.

He **prayed** and was personally prepared by the Father for 30 years of his life.

He **gathered and recruited** the core community - "come and follow me". He sought out his core community of disciples as he prepared for the onset of His ministry.

He **communicated vision** for life in the Kingdom of God. He formed the group He gathered into a community and they **lived the way** together. He not only called them for a mission. He helped them become a missional community that was loving God, loving each other and making disciples as a way of life.

He lived the way with them, **showing them the Father** by incarnating the heart of the Father through word and deed.

He taught the value of **loving relationships** with others, and how to have them. He demonstrated the heart of the Father was not the re-establishment of a religion or the start of a new religion, but in loving people.

He began to **involve** the disciples in ministry with Him and even sent them out early on in their training process.

He prayerfully identified the **"foundation stones"** or **"strategic transformers,"** the leadership community within His group which are better known as the Twelve Apostles. This shows us that Jesus sought to make disciples first, and from those disciples He then prayerfully picked His apostles. The principle here is that pastors are to first raise up disciples, and from those disciples we prayerfully select our leaders, foundations stones that provide the spiritual foundation for the work God will do in and through us. We also call them "strategic transformers" because they are able to take the vision and carry it out, "transform" it into the cultural context. These are "strategic" individuals because of their God-given calling, gifts and relational networks that will allow for the relational expansion of the faith.

From the **"foundation stones"** Jesus selected three **"catalytic leaders"**, (Peter, James and John) to accompany Him in further matters of ministry. Jesus did not select them because He liked them better or because they were more committed than the others. Rather, Jesus selected them because they were "catalytic" in their gifting and foundational to the expansion of the Gospel, as all three would play an important part in the birth and on-going development of the early church.

He **empowered and released** first the twelve and then the seventy to do ministry without Him. The "70" are undoubtedly the group or entourage that accompanied Jesus from town to town. It appears that Jesus worked more closely with three circles of relationships: Giving to the seventy, giving more to the twelve and giving even more to the three.

He **debriefed** their efforts and clarified their understanding, focusing His efforts on fully explaining the Kingdom to His core community.

The Jesus Way for Church Planting

From looking at this process of how Jesus established the first church, we gain some simple, practical insights into His process. We have distilled it here into some basic steps, not in an effort to purport some formula, but rather to illustrate the relational dynamic and process He used. Here is the pathway:

1: Recruit and gather and the core community
2: Form the community of disciples and from the core community develop leaders.
3: Live the Way together
4: Identify the gifts in your core community
5: Identify organic ministry emergence based on this gifting
6: Empower and release

Key Thought: All through this process be sure to make disciples as you go: evangelize and gather into the community. We'll say more on the implementation path for church planting later.

Principles We Learn From Jesus

Principle 1: Life-pattern teaching. Jesus lived in community (a shared life together) with His disciples. Ministry is not simply about developing competencies, or what we call discipleship to task, but about spirituality, a way of life, what we call discipleship to character. The apostle Paul said, "You should follow my example, just as I follow Christ's" (I Corinthians 11:1). Ministry is not only about what we say, but also about what we do. Our words should simply compliment the reality of our lives. As pastors and leaders we are to incarnate or show our people the way of Christianity through "life-pattern teaching."

Principle 2: If you want to start an organization, make your focus large, on the crowd. If you want to start a movement, make your focus small, on the disciples or leadership community. This is not to suggest we ignore public ministry. Jesus ministered to the crowds in word and deed (miracles). The key here is the focus of Jesus it was not on the crowds but on the Seventy and especially on the Twelve and the Three. Jesus taught the multitudes about the Kingdom, but He explained the Kingdom to His disciples.

Principle 3: Ministry is about making disciples and from those disciples developing leaders. Keep your focus on the

leadership community and not the crowd. There are then three primary circles of relationships: Relationship with the Three -- Catalytic Leaders, relationship with the Twelve -- Strategic Transformers, relationship with the Seventy: "Lay" leaders / leaders in training, and relational ministry with the Multitudes, the crowd/congregation

Principle 4: While doing public ministry with excellence do not make public ministry the focus of your investment. Rather, invest in your disciples and leaders. By investment we are referring to the use of our time currency. There are three basic types of followers to be considered for our time investment. By suggesting this time investment we are not suggesting that some people are worth more than others, but simply affirming the Jesus pattern for ministry, and the sober reality that we need to invest our relational currency in the soil that is most receptive.

The Crowd: Jesus ministered to crowds providing the Good News of the Kingdom in word and deed, healing the sick, casting out demons, etc. However, Jesus did not focus His ministry on the crowd.

The Casual Christian: This is someone who honors God in name and title, but not in devotion. From the ministry of Jesus, we see that only 25% of the seed (1 in 4) grows to fruition (See Matthew 13:18-23), and in Luke 17:17, we learn that only 10%, 1 out of the 10 lepers, responds to Jesus. What we infer from this is that 10-25% of those who hear the gospel respond and grow to be fully developed disciples of Christ. What this translates into is the 20-80 reality of the modern church where 20% of the church does 80% of the work (not true in all cases but a reality that is acknowledged and verified). What this means is that 75-90% of those who attend on Sunday mornings fall into these two categories of "crowd" or "casual" disciple. We are not casting a vote to do away with public services, Jesus ministered to the crowds and so should you in whatever format you feel called to do it. Our aim here is to learn from Jesus just exactly where we should place our focus or our investment of time.

The Core: In your leadership community you will have two

Types of disciples: Those who are "Committed" (Agenda driven) and those who are "Devoted" (Kingdom driven). It took Jesus three years to walk with his committed group of disciples who left a great deal to follow Him. However in their faith journey with Christ it becomes ever so apparent that they had an agenda. In other words, they believed that the kind of Messiah Jesus was to be was a Messiah that would come and free Israel from Roman rule and re-establish Israel in the Kingdom economy as the nation that would manifest God's glory. The disciples did not understand or believe that Jesus would go the way of the Cross, did not comprehend the kind of Messiah He was, nor how much more He had come to do not only for Israel but the entire human race, past, present and future. We learn from the ministry of Jesus that it takes radical, relational discipleship over a period of time (three years for the disciples) and a radical God encounter (death, resurrection and the Baptism of the Holy Spirit for the disciples to get it) to move the disciples from committed to devoted. All disciples, even radically committed followers of Christ according, begin the process committed, but still possess an understanding of God too small, incomplete, or agenda driven. The process of discipleship is what moves the disciple from being agenda driven (committed) to Kingdom driven (devoted).

Principle 5: All ministry is incarnational, the Immanuel Principle or "God with us." Jesus had to show them the Father.

Koinonia Means Partnership

We live in a world where koinonia or fellowship is a commodity that is in high demand but in short supply. No wonder the sitcom, *Friends,* was such a hit for ten years, as we enjoyed the relationships of six individuals who somehow, in spite of encountering great difficulties, maintained their friendships throughout the series. Their friendship translated from the silver screen into real life as the actors decided to band together and negotiate their salaries evenly. In the early stages of the show, they decided that whatever one gets paid, they all get paid. They did not like the idea of one being paid more or less than another. The show involved all six actors and all six should get equal paychecks. That is a friendship, and teamwork, and reflect rather powerfully the biblical definition of koinonia.

The biblical concept of koinonia, the basis of community, cannot take place unless there is a sense of commonality of heart and purpose, a mission that unites us. Koinonia for the Western 21st Century Christian has been reduced to potlucks or coffee and doughnuts. You know, "stay after the service and enjoy the fellowship." True fellowship can only take place where people are willing to share their lives as they share their hearts for something bigger than themselves.

This is wonderfully illustrated in Paul's relationship with the church at Philippi. The basis of Paul's thankfulness for the people at Philippi is clearly their active participation with him for the sake of the gospel (Philippians 1:3-5). The word used for partnership is "koinonia", often understood to mean fellowship. Here, it appears that it is referring to an active involvement that would include financial support.

According to Fredrich Hauck, koinonia (κοινωνία), means "participation, impartation, and fellowship" (Theological Dictionary of the New Testament, Vol. III, p. 797-798). Paul makes it clear that our fellowship begins with Jesus, "He is the one who invited you into this wonderful friendship with His Son, Jesus Christ our Lord" (I Corinthians 1:9). Koinonia thus begins with Jesus as we enter into communion or a relationship with our risen Lord, and from that relationship participate in the greater mission.

Koinonia is distinctively a Pauline word, meaning to have something common, "to give a share." It is of interest that the idea "to give a share" is rare in secular Greek. It is more common in the New Testament, especially in Paul. The word carries a wide range of ideas from describing a marital relationship to a contribution or a gift. Here, in Philippians 1:5, it is modified by "in the gospel," suggesting a partnership with an active response. Ralph

Martin states: "basically it denotes 'participation in something with someone'; and its meaning that Christians share with one another in a common possession (for example, 'the gospel' in 1:5; 'the Holy Spirit' in 2:1) is far more important than the popular modern idea of a personal association with fellow-Christians as when we use the word of a friendly atmosphere in a public meeting." (Tyndale New Testament Commentaries, The Epistle of Paul to the Philippians, Tyndale Press, Grand Rapids, MI, 1980, p 46) (Johnston & Perkinson, *N.T. Trilogy*, pp. 42-43)

True Koinonia Illustrated: The Fellowship of the Ring/Cross

Like the nine beings who volunteered for the dangerous mission in the Tolkein classic, *The Lord of the Rings*, we find ourselves in a similar situation in our world. There is an evil in our world that seeks to destroy us and most of those that inhabit earth, including many Christians, are simply unaware of the presence of this evil. God has placed it on the hearts of His people to make the journey to Mount Doom, if you will, with the **Fellowship of the Cross** to destroy the evil influence. It is a journey against unbelievable odds, enormous obstacles, and armies that outnumber and outclass us at every turn. It is the battle for our communities, cities and nation, where the liberal mindset often reigns supreme. Sin is not sin but an accepted lifestyle, and demons abide rather comfortably discouraging the church while they fan the flames of sin and evil. Our Mount Doom, like that of Tolkien's world, seems impenetrable by the likes of us. No wonder it is so easy for the believer to cower in fear or live a life of mediocrity. We applaud you, church planter, for taking on this task with your Fellowship of the Cross to undo the influence of evil and help set the captive free.

It is only in the Fellowship of the Cross that we find the full power necessary to defeat the armies of hell. Scripture makes it clear that the gates of hell cannot prevail against the church (Matthew 16:18). Jesus never said that it will be one church or a denomination, but the Church, unified in the cause of the Mission.

It's that church that hell cannot stop. Perhaps that is why Satan works so hard to keep us focused on our petty differences, to find reasons to fight and disagree, gossip, take sides, etc. If he can keep the army quarreling amongst itself it will lose its focus and destroy itself. If you have problems with someone today, then we urge you for the sake of the gospel, let it go. People will drink downstream from the waters of your life and if you have bitterness, anger, envy, jealousy, or unforgiveness, they will pollute those who drink from your life. In the greater scheme of life, especially eternal life, it's not worth it. Let it go!! Enough said, let's turn our attention back to fellowship, the biblical idea of koinonia.

Hollywood hit another koinonia homerun as they powerfully illustrated what a fellowship or koinonia is in the movie, *The Lord of the Rings: The Fellowship of the Ring*. What Tolkien's world tells us is that fellowship finds it origins in the context of mission, wherein there is a purpose, greater than ourselves or even the meeting of our own personal needs. Like the nine men in the movie, who volunteered for the dangerous mission of returning the ring to Mount Doom, we find ourselves in a similar situation in our churches and in our world. There is an evasive evil in our world that seeks to destroy us, and most of those that inhabit earth, including many Christians, are simply unaware of the danger that looms about us. God has placed it on the hearts of His people to make the journey to Mount Doom, if you will, with the fellowship (of the Cross) to destroy the evil influence (I John 3:8b). It is the battle for our families, our cities, our state, our country, and even our world. Our Mount Doom, like that of Tolkien's world, seems impenetrable by the likes of us and cannot be done by an army of one.

It is only in the Fellowship of the Cross that we find the full power necessary to defeat the armies of hell. Scripture makes it clear that the gates of hell cannot prevail against the Church (Matthew 16:18). Jesus never said that it will be one church or a denomination that will be able to resist hell, but the Church, unified in the cause of the Mission.

True Koinonia Begins with Sacrifice

The problem that many have, and you will as well as a church planter, within the realm of today's Christian society is that we have not allowed ourselves to be crucified with Christ. We often choose a life of self-protection and self-advancement over the Kingdom of God. When such takes place in the life of a Christian, and particularly a church planter, love for the things of God begins to grow cold and die. In its place we find such things as caring for people as a means to an end, and justify it with the language of vision and mission. We pastor for our benefit and focus on the trappings of the meal without ever serving or living the meal (the gospel). So much of our Christian life is based around trying to get God to bless our lives and make them better. The problem is that we often want the blessing instead of God.

The nominal state of so many believers, including pastors and leaders, is alarming and even discouraging. Embracing God's rule in our lives, becoming radical and real followers of Christ involves taking up one's cross. True fellowship begins with Jesus as we take up our crosses and follow him. Jesus said, *"If any of you wants to be my follower, you must put aside your selfish ambition, shoulder your cross daily, and follow me"* (Luke 9:23).

Exactly what does it mean to take up one's cross? So much of what we call crosses in our Christian vernacular have nothing to do with the cross that Jesus referred to. For example, our problems with people, trials, sicknesses, etc., might be difficult matters for us in life, but have very little to do with taking up your cross. **The cross is not a burden. Rather, it is a place of death**. When one is willing to take up the cross, they are ready to die. We are not talking about denying oneself of various things (as good as this is for practicing spiritual discipline), but to deny oneself, to give up rulership of your life and submit to the one who is King. **Self-denial is centered upon the self; to deny the self is centered upon Christ**. It is the language of personal death to one's dreams, ambitions, and desires. Cross-bearing deals with the question of lordship, rulership, and kingship. Christ cannot rule in one's life until one considers themselves as dead, crucified with Him. As Paul boldly asserts, *"I myself no longer live, but Christ lives in me. So I live my life in this earthly body by trusting in the Son of God, who loved me and gave himself for me"* (Galatians 2:20).

Practically, this means that we do not dictate to God the terms of our involvement, the "I don't do windows" mentality that is so often found in the household of the faith. It's almost as if our gift assessments and personal mission statements have allowed us to skirt the issue of being servants. "I am a servant, but I just don't do windows. I can serve in the following ways based upon my gifts and personal mission statement." Now before you decide to blow a fuse, We are all for gift assessments and discovering your personal mission statement, but reflect a moment on how such practices, without serious cross-bearing, will lead to a language of biblical faith without the love and humility of biblical faith. When such transpires, we have those who serve only when it is within their comfort or best interest. After all, if it doesn't fit my personal mission statement or gifts, then I simply do not have to do it. Koinonia begins with fellowship with Jesus occurs when one takes up one's cross and follows Him.

John Harper was born to a pair of solid Christian parents on May 29th, 1872. It was on the last Sunday of March 1886, when he was thirteen years old that he received Jesus as the Lord of his life. He never knew what it was to "sow his wild oats." He began to preach about four years later at the ripe old age of seventeen years by going down to the streets of his village and pouring out his soul in earnest entreaty for men to be reconciled to God.

As John Harper's life unfolded, one thing was apparent: he was consumed by the Word of God. When asked by various ministers what his doctrine consisted of, he was known to reply, "The Word of God!" After five or six years of toiling on street corners preaching the gospel and working in the mill during the day, Harper was taken in by E. A. Carter of Baptist Pioneer Mission in London, England. This set Harper free to devote his whole time and energy to the work so dear to his heart. Soon, John Harper started his own church in September of 1896, now known as the Harper Memorial Church. This church, which he had started with just twenty-five members, had grown to over five hundred members when he left thirteen years later. During this time he had gotten married and God did bless John Harper with a beautiful little girl named Nana.

Ironically, John Harper almost drowned several times during his life. When he was two and a half years of age, he almost drowned when he fell into a well but was resuscitated by his mother. At twenty-six, he was swept out to sea by a reverse current and barely survived, and at thirty-two he faced death on a leaking ship in the Mediterranean. Perhaps God used these experiences to prepare His servant for what he faced next.

It was the night of April 14, 1912. RMS Titanic sailed swiftly on the bitterly cold ocean waters, heading unknowingly into the pages of history. On board this luxurious ocean liner were many rich and famous people. At the time of the ship's launch, it was the world's largest man-made moveable object. At 11:40 p.m. on that fateful night, an iceberg scraped the ship's starboard side, showering the decks with ice and ripping open six watertight compartments. The sea poured in.

On board the ship that night was John Harper and his much-beloved six-year-old daughter, Nana. According to documented reports, as soon as it was apparent that the ship was going to sink, Harper immediately took his daughter to a lifeboat. It is reasonable to assume that this widowed preacher could have easily gotten on board this boat to safety; however, it never seems to have crossed his mind. He bent down and kissed his precious little girl; looking into her eyes he told her that she would see him someday. The flares going off in the dark sky above reflected the tears on his face as he turned and headed towards the crowd of desperate humanity on the sinking ocean liner. As the rear of the huge ship began to lurch upwards, it was reported that Harper was seen making his way up the deck yelling, "Women, children, and unsaved into the lifeboats!" It was only minutes later that the Titanic began to rumble deep within. Most people thought it was an explosion; actually the gargantuan ship was literally breaking in half. At this point, many people jumped off the decks and into the icy, dark waters below. John Harper was one of these people.

That night 1528 people went into the frigid waters. Harper was seen swimming frantically to people in the water leading them to Jesus before the hypothermia became fatal. Mr. Harper swam up to one young man who had climbed up on a piece of debris. Rev. Harper asked him between breaths, "Are you saved?" The young man replied that he was not.

Harper then tried to lead him to Christ only to have the young man, who was near shock, reply "No." John Harper then took off his life jacket and threw it to the man and said, "Here then, you need this more than I do." And swam away to other people. A few minutes later Harper swam back to the young man and succeeded in leading him to salvation. Of the 1528 people that went into the water that night, six were rescued by the lifeboats. One of them was this young man on the debris. Four years later, at a survivors meeting, this young man stood up and in tears recounted how that after John Harper had led him to Christ, Mr. Harper had tried to swim back to help other people, yet because of the intense cold, had grown too weak to swim. His last words before going under in the frigid waters were, "Believe on the Name of the Lord Jesus and you will be saved."

Does Hollywood remember this man? No. No matter! This servant of God did what he had to do. While other people were trying to buy their way onto the lifeboats and selfishly trying to save their own lives, John Harper gave up his life so that others could be saved.

"Greater love hath no man that this, that he lay down his life for his friends". John Harper was truly the hero of the Titanic! **True koinonia begins when we take up our crosses and lay down our lives, living for something more than ourselves.** (Taken from "The Titanic's Last Hero" by Moody Press 1997, Scriptures are quoted from the King James Bible. Source: Monday Fodder http://www.witandwisdom.org)

Chapter Six R.E.A.D. Questions - "Who is Your Community?"

R -

- Based on your *reflection*, list the three major things that the Holy Spirit spoke to your heart regarding the life and ministry of Jesus.
- *Reflect* on your current process of ministering like Jesus.
- *Reflect* on how you relate to people as human beings and not human doings.
- *Reflect* on your discipling process. Your leadership development process.

E -

- Based on the new awareness that you have gained, how would you *evaluate* your current life and church plant in relationship to how Jesus did ministry?
- *Evaluate* how your life reflects the relational process of Jesus that formed disciples and developed leaders and started a movement.
- *Evaluate* how your church plant will disciple people in Kingdom fruitfulness.

A -
What do you need to *adjust* on each of the above?

D -
What will you *do* about it?

CHAPTER 7 – WHERE ARE YOU CALLED?

Jesus wants to send you ahead of him to the locality where he desires to move in a new way. This is what he did in Luke 10:

> *After this the Lord appointed seventy-two others and sent them on ahead of him, two by two, into every town and place where he himself was about to go. And he said to them, "The harvest is plentiful, but the laborers are few. Therefore pray earnestly to the Lord of the harvest to send out laborers into his harvest (Luke 10:1-2).*

There is a harvest of souls and Jesus wants to gather it. To that end he is sending you to a town, city or region which He wants to impact with His grace. This is your quest – to bring the Gospel of the Kingdom to the ends of the earth. You are His laborer, and He has a field for you to till. But where, specifically, should you start this new church? Does it really matter what location you choose. Yes, we think it does, and that's what we want to highlight in the next few pages.

During his first planting project, Tom was trying to discern where the Lord wanted him to establish the church. Initially, he was drawn to the largest city in his state, drawn by the density of population and the apparent low percentage of that population involved in a church. After a season of prayer and reflection, Tom felt the Lord's resistance to this city as the location to start the church. Since he was being sent out from a church in the second largest city – and planting there wasn't in consideration, he began to look at the third largest city. This choice seemed to have potential as well – a college town which was growing and had a very low percentage of the population in attendance in a church. The Lord shut the door on this one as well. Perplexed by his apparent inability to hear God on the subject of location, Tom and his wife Cathy went into a season of prayer. Clarity came while visiting a piece of property some friends had purchased in a small town, where they would be building their new home. It became clear to Tom and Cathy almost immediately that this small town of five thousand people was the place to start the new work. God just reached out and grabbed their hearts, wiping away all preconceptions of where this church would be, and therefore what the church would be like. The selection of this area as the planting target defied the conventional wisdom on the subject, ignoring the demographics, trusted to the intuitive leading of the Holy Spirit.

The church plant took off. Within forty days of moving to the town, knowing no one (their friends had not built the house yet), they established relationships that sparked a core team being developed, with a public worship gathering being started the following year. People came to Jesus, a church building was built – and Tom and Cathy learned to pastor. That was sixteen years ago. From that humble beginning a state-wide church planting movement was started, as people we converted and empowered for ministry. From this first plant, four church planters were developed and sent out. The first daughter church was in that third largest city Tom had considered, and Tom and Cathy's third personal church plant and the church they currently pastor is in that first largest city he had originally wanted to target. A total of nine church plants came from this original beginning – four planted personally, three daughter churches (one being in Russia) and two granddaughter churches. As it has turned out, God knew what He was doing in sending Tom & Cathy to that small town. It was a goldmine for church planters and pastors.

Paul had a similar situation when his missionary team tried to enter Asia and then Bithynia, and the Spirit of God resisted him. Instead, he was led of the Lord to go to Macedonia (Acts

16:6-10). From this Lyida was saved and the church at Philippi was established (Acts 16:12).

> *And they went through the region of Phrygia and Galatia, having been forbidden by the Holy Spirit to speak the word in Asia. And when they had come up to Mysia, they attempted to go into Bithynia, but the Spirit of Jesus did not allow them. So, passing by Mysia, they went down to Troas. And a vision appeared to Paul in the night: a man of Macedonia was standing there, urging him and saying, "Come over to Macedonia and help us." And when Paul had seen the vision, immediately we sought to go on into Macedonia, concluding that God had called us to preach the gospel to them (Acts 16:6-01 ESV).*

Having a sense of divine call to a location or people group is essential in seeing a planting project prosper. Simply planting based on demographics or a regional strategy leaves the planter vulnerable. Without a divine imperative driving their mission, two things could happen. A commitment based on divine call empowers the planter to stand in the midst of adversity. The certainty of being called by God to a location or people group stiffens the spiritual spine. The enemy will bring adversity, and you will question your calling at some point. Planting based on demographics or someone's well-intentioned strategy leaves us open to the question the enemy loved "Did God really say?" Having a clear sense that God has called us to a particular place allows us to say, 'Yes, He did!"

The second thing this can affect is the understanding of our partnership with God. We want to do what we see Him doing (John 5:19) and participate with Him in that (1 Corinthians 3:6-9). Without a sense that God wants to do something *specific* in a particular *location*, it would be hard to track with Him in undertaking ministry that would facilitate His will emerging.

The question becomes "How do we know where we are called to?" The answer lies in the transformation of our minds.

> *I appeal to you therefore, brothers, by the mercies of God, to present your bodies as a living sacrifice, holy and acceptable to God, which is your spiritual worship. Do not be conformed to this world, but be transformed by the renewal of your mind, that by testing you may discern what is the will of God, what is good and acceptable and perfect. (Romans 12:1-2 ESV).*

Personal renewal always precedes corporate renewal. Change must come to us personally before we can facilitate change in the Kingdom economy. Having our internal framework renewed in a way that pleases the Father allows us to hear His voice more clearly, and discern more specifically, His path for us in life. If we are conformed to this world in our thinking – in this application, by basing our decisions and consequent actions on presuppositions of where we should plant – then we will continually miss God's intention for both our life and ministry. We submit our attitude, thinking and the resultant ministry process of church planting to Him by surrendering our preconceptions. We must do this in all things, but first and foremost in determining where to start this new church. We must allow Him to speak, beyond our emotions, our desires and our preconceptions of what this church will look like.

How do we do that? First, *pray.* Simple enough, right? Pray and ask the Lord to direct your heart and your thoughts. You probably have some sense already what it is the Lord wants you to do, and a basic framework for where He wants you to establish the church. Where or to whom is He drawing your heart? Jesus' daily discipline of prayer kept targeting what He would do in carrying out ministry. His focus was to see what the Father was doing and to do likewise (John 5:19). To this end, he sought the Father continually. One really good snapshot of the impact of this kind of prayer is seen in Mark 1:

> *And rising very early in the morning, while it was still dark, he departed and went out to a desolate place, and there he*

> *prayed. And Simon and those who were with him searched for him, and they found him and said to him, "Everyone is looking for you." And he said to them, "Let us go on to the next towns, that I may preach there also, for that is why I came out." And he went throughout all Galilee, preaching in their synagogues and casting out demons (Mark 1:35-39).*

Jesus received and maintained His focus from prayer. While we could argue here that all ministry efforts must be birthed from prayer, our main intent is to show that guidance in application to His missionary journeys came from the place of prayer. Here, too, we find the model of Jesus is our example as well. Locating the place God wants you to plant His church starts first in the place of prayer.

Second, **discern your motives**. Ask the Holy Spirit to clarify your thoughts and feelings concerning the potential location or people group you are seeking to reach for Jesus. Is there anything within yourself influencing your desire to plant the church within the specific geography or people group, anything based in a human need of your own? Planters have sought to plant churches in a specific location for many wrong reasons: "It's close to family;" "the cost of living is lower there;" "there are lots of Christians there already looking for a church like ours." Check your heart and make sure you are looking at a specific location for all the right reasons: God's heart breaks yours for the city.

David Wilkerson is an excellent example of a man with a calling to a place. Here is an excerpt from his life relating to his call to New York City.

> *The whole strange adventure got its start one night as I sat in my study reading Life magazine. I merely turned a page, and at first glance it seemed there was nothing to interest me. The page showed a pen drawing of a trial taking place in New York City, 350 miles away from my home in rural Pennsylvania. I'd never been to New York, and I'd never*

wanted to go, except perhaps to see the Statue of Liberty.

I started to flip the page over. But as I did, something caught my eye. It was the eyes of a figure in the drawing – a boy. He was one of seven boys on trial for murder. I held the magazine closer to get a better look. The artist had captured a look of bewilderment, hatred and despair in the young boy's features. Suddenly, I began to cry.

"What's the matter with me?" I wondered, impatiently brushing away a tear. Then I looked at the picture more carefully. The boys were all teenagers. They were members of a gang called the Dragons. Beneath the picture was the story of how they had been in Highbridge Park in New York when they brutally attacked and killed a fifteen-year-old polio victim named Michael Farmer.

The story revolted me. It literally turned my stomach. In our little mountain town, such things seemed mercifully unbelievable. Yet I was dumbfounded by the next thought that sprang into my head. It came to me full-blown, as if from somewhere else: Go to New York and help those boys.

The thought startled me. "I'd be a fool to do that," I reasoned. "I know nothing about kids like these. And I don't want to know anything."

It was no use. The idea wouldn't go away. I was to go to New York. And I was to do it at once, while the trial was still in progress.

This trip changed his life forever. David Wilkerson's burden for the lost of the city increased and gave birth to Teen Challenge – a nationwide ministry to reach out to people with life controlling habits. The ministry's Bible-based recovery program to troubled teens, gang members, drug addicts and alcoholics has been recognized as one of the most effective efforts of its kind. (Taken from David Wilkerson's website http://www. davidwilkerson.org/

hislife/)

When God calls you to the place of His choosing, when He touches your heart, miracles can and will happen, with transformed lives as a result.

Next, **do some research.** Don't just go on prepackaged demographics: Get out into the street and meet people. Seeing how the people live will help you understand if this is the place where Jesus wants to incarnate a new local church community through you. This is not market research that you are doing as some part of a business plan; *it is heart research*, finding out if God is connecting your heart with this people specifically.

One planter we know did some man-on-the-street interviews as part of his discernment process. He went on into the street, along with a ministry partner and a video camera. He simply stopped people on the street and asked some simple questions about their perception of God, their church involvement and what they would want in a church if they were to attend one. His interaction with the men and women he was interviewing did confirm his general sense to plant the church in the location he was considering, but it did much more. Through his connection with the harvest field, God touched his heart and gave him a passion for the people, *His passion*. For all of us, the Father's heart of love and compassion for a unique people and place is what we need lay hold of. This is the only way for us to truly affirm a calling of God. Get out into the target culture you are seeking to impact, and encounter the harvest. See it, smell it, taste it, touch it. The harvest is not always obvious to us. Sometimes we have spiritual blinders on, not being able to see the harvest for all of the people. Jesus' disciples had this issue, In John 4. Jesus had just had His classic dialog with the woman at the well in Samaria. She had gone into the town, shared her experience with Jesus and the whole town was streaming out to see this man would could be the Christ. In the midst of this, entered the clueless Twelve, trying to feed Jesus lunch. They were astonished that he would speak to this woman, a Samaritan no less. Caught up with the needs of the moment, and not being able to see beyond the cultural barriers, they missed seeing the potential in this situation. Jesus finally has to point the opportunity out:

> Do you not say, 'There are yet four months, then comes the harvest'? Look, I tell you, lift up your eyes, and see that the fields are white for harvest. (John 4:35 ESV.)

Jesus' encouragement was to see the current reality in light of the Kingdom quest. These people coming en mass to see Jesus were the harvest. The harvest was *now*, right in front of them, and not a future dynamic yet to come. So it is with us. There is a harvest in every city, town or region, and in every generation. The fields are white, so ask the Lord to show you where to start this new church community: ask Him to open your eyes to the abundance of souls around you.

This brings us to our last point in discerning the location for your new church. **Ask God for vision**. Ask Him to form in you a picture of His preferred future for that community you are considering. Let Him set your heart and mind ablaze with the picture of what the local society could look like transformed by the Gospel. Pray and ask Him to liberate your thinking from the limitations of what you know so that you can see the potential of what can be. As you do this, He will unfold in your heart what this new church community will look like: you'll see it and how its mission can impact the city. Once you connect at this level with God's heart and intention for a locality, once you get a glimpse of the need and then see how the resource of Jesus can meet it, then you can know that you are hot on the trail of God's plan and purpose for planting in the area you are considering. When you can see it, when He opens you heart and mind to perceive His will, then you can proceed to the next step: developing the foundation of your community. And that is where we want to take you next.

Chapter Seven R.E.A.D. Questions - "Where Are You Called To?"

R -

- Based on your *reflection*, list the three major things that the Holy Spirit spoke to your heart regarding the geography or people group He is calling you to.
- *Reflect* on your current process of discernment concerning your planting target geography.
- *Reflect* on additional ways to seek Him in this process.
- *Reflect* on your motives for church planting in this particular location.

E -

- Based on the new awareness that you have gained, how would you *evaluate* your current life and church plant in relationship to the people you are seeking to reach.
- *Evaluate* how your life reflects the current culture.
- *Evaluate* how your church plant will connect with these people? What would "good news" be to these people?

A -

What do you need to *adjust* on each of the above?

D -

What <u>will</u> you *do* about it?

CHAPTER 8 - HOW WILL YOU FORM THIS NEW COMMUNITY?

In Mike's first church plant he was 26 years old when the core community began to meet with the understanding that they were going to plant a church. It was a young group of eager believers that wanted to do something with their lives in reaching Orange County in Southern California. This was back in 1986 when very little literature existed about church planting, and so Mike and his young team began to prayerfully process who they would be and how that would be reflected in their core community.

Mike and the co-pastor sat down at a Burger King and talked through what the philosophy and developmental process of the church would be. In other words, who they would be as a church and what would they do to people that came to their church. A leadership flow chart was developed for clarity, specifying gift assignments and roles.

From that point Mike and his team worked to develop the people according to the values, although they did not call them values at the time, that Mike and his key associate held and by doing the values to the people as well as teaching them through bible study and seminars. The focus was not on the public launch as much as it was on who they were going to be as a people. The team not only learned about community but watched the key leaders model Christianity, friendship, community and relationship. The core community gradually became infected by the values, resulting in heart and lifestyle changes which allowed for relational connection and community to be fostered. By the launch of the public service over one hundred people had been developed and a solid community of believers became a Fellowship of the Cross on mission to make disciples in Orange County.

Key to Formation: "Do as I Do and as I Say"

Church planter, as you begin this church plant be sure to remember that the key to developing and forming disciples is found in John 1:14 wherein the apostle John tells us that the Word, Jesus, became flesh and pitched his tent or lived amongst us – the Incarnation: Immanuel where Jesus came to live with us and showed us the Father. What we mean is that you will need to live out your values with your core community, incarnating or pitching your tent with your people to show them the way as Christ is showing you the way. It is more important that you model Christianity to your people, rather than how to attend a church service. Remember, you are modeling a way of life, developing people as Christians (Discipleship to Character) as well as developing them in their gift understanding, capacity and assignment (Discipleship to Task). As the old adage so profoundly states, "More is caught than taught."

You are building this church upon the foundation of the apostles and prophets (Ephesians 2:20), that is a life lived out in submission to the One who was crucified and resurrected on the third day; a life, your life that daily reflects this death to self as you daily clothe yourself with the new nature of Christ that has been graciously given you.

> *In its place you have clothed yourselves with a brand-new nature that is continually being renewed as you learn more and more about Christ, who created this new nature within you. In this new life, it doesn't matter if you are a*

Jew or a Gentile, circumcised or uncircumcised, barbaric, uncivilized, slave, or free. Christ is all that matters, and he lives in all of us. (Colossians 3:10-11, NLT)

What matters in life is Christ and how your church plant reflects Christ as a people called out to love God, love each other and make disciples (doing this all together) is the heart and soul of the Church.

The questions you will want to answer in this life to life process are as follows.
- How will you love God?
- How will you love others?
- How will you make disciples as you go?

Having answered the above questions allows you to know what you will do to the people that are part of your core community. The key function of your role is to equip your people to do this (Ephesians 4:11-16). The development process that you will want to develop can be found as you answer the questions below. As you provide answers to these questions, the framework for your discipleship pathway will begin to emerge, which will be the guiding framework for the development of the people.

- How will we develop people in their love for God? What will be the process or pathway for this?
- How will we develop people in their love for each other? What will be the process or pathway for this?
- How will we develop people to become disciple makers as a way of life? What will be the process or pathway for this?

"You Cannot Reproduce What You Cannot Incarnate"

One of our good friends, Al Soto, who pastors in San Jose, California, made the comment during a teaching that "you cannot reproduce what you cannot incarnate," a powerful truth vital for your young church to grasp. The point of the teaching is that whatever you are living out is what you will reproduce. You cannot reproduce something by simply speaking it in a classroom. It has to be fostered in the world of relationship and real life. When a husband and wife want to have a child, it will not happen if they simply read books on parenting, review baby names, build their nursery and even pray over the process. We all know what must take place for reproduction.

Unless we incarnate the reality of Jesus with our lives, they will not reproduce. Words should illustrate and illuminate the reality of our life in Jesus. On a negative note, what will be reproduced is what you are living out, not necessarily what you are verbally teaching. For example, if you are teaching your people to be Jesus to the world, to love and care for others, serving their needs while you are ignoring your people's needs all the while attempting to meet the needs of those outside the faith. Over time, your people will learn that love is about task, loving those on the outside while ignoring those on the inside. When you are on the outside, it is great, but once you enter the internal world you find the reality far different than the one encountered, and ultimately, expected. Suddenly, you feel like a means to an end and the lies of hell begin to torment you and set you up for disaffection and disillusionment with the church and even with God.

The inception or beginning of the church plant is significant because you can establish the environment that allows life to form around your DNA (values). This is transmitted relationally (life to life) with your core community as you do your values to the core community, and with them, showing them the way of Jesus. As you incarnate the reality of Jesus, you will find that reality reproducing and impacting life all around you and beyond.

Establishing and Maintaining the Environment

To help us form this new community lets take a look at

ecology. In ecology, the word ecosystem is an abbreviation of the term, ecological system, and some consider this the basic unit of the science.

In general terms, an ecological system can be thought of as an assemblage of organisms (plant, animal and other living organism, also referred to as a biotic community or biocoenosis), living together with their environment, their biotope, functioning as a loose unit. It is a dynamic and complex whole, interacting as an "ecological unit".

The ecological unit is understood to be a structured functional unit in equilibrium. In this view, an ecological a functional organization in *dynamic equilibrium* or what is also referred to as *steady state*, the phase of an ecological system's development when the organisms are in harmony with each other and their environment.

The role of the pastor is then to facilitate life by creating an environment that allows for the various ecosystems, to connect and find their *steady state* wherein life is maximized, harmonized (unity), and the fullness of God finds expression through the body of believers called the Church.

It should be noted that in our world, the size and scale of an ecosystem can vary widely. An ecosystem may be a whole forest, as well as a small pond. Different ecosystems are often separated by geographical barriers such as deserts, mountains or oceans, or find themselves isolated as is the case with like lakes or rivers. The borders of these ecosystems are never rigid which means that ecosystems tend to blend into each other. As a result, the earth as a whole can be seen as a single ecosystem, which speaks powerfully on what the Church is to be, One Ecosystem with many ecosystems within. Theologically we have called this the Church Universal and the Church Local.

What this means for us today is that all too often our churches function more like biospheres than as parts of the ecological whole. The earth is an ecosystem in and of itself as well as having many ecosystems within the whole. As a biosphere, the church closes itself off from the Ecosystem (the

Church as a whole), and creates its own ecosystem for survival. As a biosphere, the church is then isolated from the ecological whole, the environment. For the Church to be the Church, Jesus said that the gates of Hell cannot stand against it, we must become part of the ecological whole one Ecosystem – or should we say the ecclesiological whole, being one in Christ for the purpose of His glory, sharing His life and love as we live our lives for Him.

It is very important that you do not underestimate the power of the environment in your church plant. The atmosphere the Lord uses you to create is much of the ministry dynamic that will facilitate the outworking of your mission. Healing and wholeness come through exposure to the One who is whole, the One who is our Healer. He is embodied in His people, the Church, and moves in the relational fabric, the incarnational environment of the local church community. It is this environment that enriches and empowers people, through the totality of a church's life and mission. Therefore, focus not only on what you as a church will do, but who you are as a people of God as well. This is part of your quest to bring the Kingdom near to people, building an environment within your church community that gives life, the life of Jesus Christ.

Developing the Core Community

Let us recap what we have said thus far. We have said that Christianity is incarnational, relational or life to life, that Church is about the "irreducible core" of loving God, loving others and making disciples, and that Christianity is a way of life, not simply a series of religious meetings.

In Luke 10:1-9, we find the basis for our understanding on how one should go about recruiting the core community. As you begin the process of recruiting and forming your core community, you will want to **identify the oikos** (Luke 10:1-9) that will be the basis by which the heart and soul of your church plant will begin. Oikos is the Greek word for "house" or "household" (see, Acts 10:22 – Cornelius; Acts 16:15 – Lydia; Acts 16:31-36 - Philippian jailer; Acts 18:7-9 – Crispus). By identifying the oikos, you finding a family that is open to you, the Gospel and the vision God has placed on your heart.

Second, you will want to **connect the roots** relationally with people. What we mean by this is that any two people are connected by only six degrees of separation, so it only takes five redemptive connections to reach the world! People know people, and as you love them and provide the miraculous presence of Christ in their lives, you will find amazing opportunities to connect with others they know as they open up their relational network to you.

Let's take a moment to look at what you should do when you building your core community.

The first is **pray**. How often should you pray? As a church planter, you'll discover that it will be all the time. Fall on your knees daily and "Beg the Lord for workers for the harvest (Matthew 9:37-38). Our friend Neil Cole often says "Woo the Groom to give birth to the church." The general rule of church planting is pray, pray, pray!!!

Second look for places where people hang out, places where non-believers socialize and live, like your job. You may want to become part of a community endeavor, help coach a local sports team for kids, join a gym, etc. In Mike's first church plant, most of his core community was recruited where he worked. Mike was going to seminary and working a part time job at a shoe store where he was able to lead twelve people to Christ who then became a part of the core community of the new church. You know your job often provides you with wonderful opportunities to be in people's lives, to love them, pray for them, and incarnate Jesus. We have found that, over time, it is hard for people to resist Jesus, a Jesus that loves, accepts and forgives. Keep in mind that one of the greatest techniques for evangelization is being a good Christian. That is one who loves God, loves people and makes disciples as a way of life.

Next is look for and expect His presence because He is with you. Another favorite comment from our friend Neil Cole is "You bring the presence of the King with you. Where you go, the King goes and where the King goes people bow." Jesus instructed the disciples that "As you go, preach this message: 'The kingdom of heaven is near.' Heal the sick, raise the dead, cleanse those who have leprosy, drive out demons. Freely you have received, freely give." (Matthew 10:7-8)

The fourth step is seek out the "person of peace." Jesus tells us

> "When you enter a house (oikos), first say 'Peace to this house (oikos). If a man of peace is there, your peace will rest on him; if not, it will return to you. Stay in that house (oikos), eating and drinking whatever they give you, for the worker deserves his wages. Do not move around from house (oikos) to house (oikos)." (Luke 10:5-7)

The person of peace is someone who will help connect you with others, who will open the door relationally for you to enter the lives of other people. The person of peace is someone who is responsive to the message you bring, is relationally connected and quickly shares Christ with those in his/her network. They have a renowned reputation, an established reputation. This reputation can be one that is good or bad, and doesn't matter necessarily, but he or she will be someone who is known.

Gathering Your First Harvest

So, you connect with the person of peace, people are impacted with the Gospel, lives are changed as men, women and children give themselves to Christ. Those people who are part of your core community working with you are excited to see Jesus on the move, and everyone asks you, "Now what?" It's time to gather the flock.

At this juncture let's just hit the pause button for a minute. What we just said is that you should gather people together. Here's what we didn't say: We didn't say "Start a Sunday morning church service." We didn't say anything about "worship", or music or programs or advertising or buildings. You see, the danger here is that you are standing at the beginning of a wave of the moving God's Spirit, and instead of riding that wave and seeing the unique places God wants to take you and your new church community, you may very well kill the thing dead by getting all religious. What do we mean? The default position for most planters in thinking about what this church is going to look like when it is formed usually falls into one or more of four groups: **the last church experience, the anti-church, the dream church** and **the cool church.** Let's break each one of these down a bit.

A planter, who has a positive, highly formative experience of a church, perhaps one they are even being sent from, may have the tendency to **want to recreate their last church experience.** The life of Christ they experienced in their last church was wonderful, and they want everyone they come in contact with to have the same thing; and as great as the planter's personal experience was, they running on "Christian memory" from their past. Unfortunately, in a new location with new people who have no connection with the planter's experience or with Christianity, this can be a very limiting error – you end up reaching only a slice of the population. This is not spiritual reproduction; it's cloning. Jesus isn't into that; He's into the new birth (John 3:3). He wants to give birth through you. The church is a living thing, not an organization that can be franchised. You're not a business, you're a family that is growing and expanding. Although many of the things you carry within you as part of your spiritual DNA may well come from a positive church experience, the Lord wants to take that and shape in into something that may be similar, but still in and of itself a unique living organism. So, repeat with us, "No, clones!" Let Him be big and creative in you.

The next major default position is just the opposite. This one comes from the planter's negative experience, trying to redress the wrongs they have suffered or have seen others suffer. From this we get **the anti-church,** the one designed to fix all the problems with the church over the past 2000 years. Tom knew a planter who started a church this way, building the foundation of the new work on "anti." When the planter expressed his values for the church, they came in statements of what the church was **not** going to be, rather than who they already were as people. The work never prospered under his leadership. A new pastor was brought in, one with a different spirit, and the church doubled in a few months.

If you are angry at the church, if you have been wounded, get healed by Jesus **before** planting. Let go of the anger. We like what Yoda says: "Anger leads to hate. Hate leads to suffering." Jesus, in contrasting Himself with the evil one said this: "The thief comes only to steal and kill and destroy. I came that they may have life and have it abundantly (John 10:10 ESV)."

Anything you build on "anti" will only bring death to people. Jesus wants to give them life. Building an anti-church is just all about the planter (or their core community if the group as a whole is infected with the same horrible virus). It is for them a way of venting their spiritual spleen. Such an endeavor is doomed to be self-focused and not God and other focused. It also opens a subtle door to too many dark things to discuss here. Check your heart. Being angry at the church is being angry at Jesus' bride. Bad plan. You could find yourself interceding against the people of God, like Elijah. It cost him his job (1 Kings 19:16). You might even find your self in agreement with the Accuser of the Brethren (Revelation 12:10). Double bad plan. Give birth to the church Jesus wants, the one which gives away His life, vitality and hope. People will be hurt in churches because other people are there. It can't be escaped. Some things in the church in each generation will need to change, and we can learn from the past mistakes of others. Be a reformer, even a revolutionary, but don't try to make a new wineskin by attacking the older one. It got you, and all of us, to where we are in Christ today.

The third default position is building **the church you've always dreamed of**, but have never seen. You're full of vision, full of hope. You're not hurt or angry at anybody, and you have a heart to build the First Church of Heaven on Earth. And you know **exactly** what it will be like, the worship, the meetings, the preaching, even the kind people; you know, they are kind, they are the teachable, faithful committed ones all of whom tithe 20%. You have it mapped out in the smallest degree. It is all neatly bound together in a 300 page manual, with demographics, PERT charts, flow diagrams and budget. You've got it all locked down. You even have a PowerPoint presentation burned onto a CDROM tucked neatly into a specially designed pocket inside the front cover. All of this is precisely the problem: You've planned out what will happen so well you don't even need God. To pull off this ideal church you will need everything to happen just as you have imagined. There is no room for error, no place for mistakes – or for imperfect people. You will need each member to relate with others *only* in the fruit of the Spirit and perform their pre-determined, pre-assigned ministry task with robotic precision. The leader of this kind of church is not a pastor, but a puppet-master, pulling everyone's string and calling all the shots.

How do you avoid this one? Just accept that this church, indeed all churches, will be made up of broken, imperfect people, just like you. Implementation planning is hugely important, as is getting the Spirit-driven plan on paper. But don't forget the grace factor; that thing the church is all about. Jerry Cook says that the church should be a refuge for imperfect people. People will mess up and you can't control that. Like we always say, all control is an illusion. The question is; can broken, lost and hopeless people find the Grace of God in Jesus Christ through your faith community? If so, then that's what Jesus' dream church looks like. Build that one.

Finally, we come to the last of our four pitfalls, **the cool church syndrome.** This one is all about the wineskin. The belief is "if we build it, and it is cool enough, they will come." The focus here is on style, with the thought being that by doing proper cultural exegesis we can determine the societal triggers we need to pull to get people to come and hear the message of the Kingdom. The problem is obvious: Style is not the issue in the church of Jesus Christ, substance is. It is not about the container; it's about the contents. A paper cup or a ceramic mug doesn't affect the flavor of the coffee; it just may either enhance or detract from the experience of drinking the coffee, depending on the style preferences of the drinker. Paper cups don't seem to inhibit Starbucks (one of our favorite writing places) in their charging way too much for an Americano (four shots, one Splenda, no room) or a White Chocolate Mocha (skim, with whip). It's about the beans; it's about what makes good coffee. And now they even have drive-thru windows (what's with that?), so it's not just about the experience. People go there first for the coffee, then for the ambiance. There is some good content in those paper cups.

As you gather your new harvest of souls together, it's not about how cool the church is. It's about how much Jesus you have to give away, the content of your life together as a community. Coolness is highly subjective. What is cool in one area or one cultural setting is bizarre in another. Focus on the content, allowing it to emerge within the culture. The church will incarnate within the society it is being birthed into, so whatever that looks like is OK. It might be cool, it might not. It all depends on your point of view. What is essential is this, that the presence of Jesus be found in it – no matter what it looks like.

OK, the pause button is off. So, all that being said, now what are you going to do? How will this new community gather? Are you ready to decide how this new family in Christ will meet? Do you want us to tell you? Sorry! We wish we could, but we can't, because we don't know. We know what we would do where we are with the people we have been given to care for in Jesus. We know how we would disciple them. You have to make that choice for yourself, not Rick Warren or Bill Hybells or Wayne Codierro or even Ralph Moore (sorry Ralph). We can't help you here, but we know Someone who can.

How you gather, what the church looks like and how it functions can be as simple or as complex as it needs to be, all in line with how Jesus has chosen to express Himself in and through the people of your core community. Look at who you are, your values. Look at what you see God doing through your church, your vision. Look at what He wants to accomplish through your band of adventurers, your mission. All that flows together into determining what the form or structure of your church, its ministries and gatherings, will look like. That is an answer you will have to wrestle out of Jesus Himself, for it is He who is building His church (Matthew 16:18). What matters here is that you do decide how you will gather, and that you do gather and live together as a community with Jesus in the midst.

Chapter Eight R.E.A.D. Questions -
"How Will You Form This New Community?"

R -

- Based on your *reflection*, list the three major things that the Holy Spirit spoke to your heart regarding the formation of your community.
- *Reflect* on your current process of developing people.
- *Reflect* on how you disciple people to character and to task.
- *Reflect* on your discipling process. Your leadership development process.

E -

- Based on the new awareness that you have gained, how would you *evaluate* your current developmental processes of spiritual formation?
- *Evaluate* how you love God, love others and make disciples as you.
- *Evaluate* how your church is doing in loving God, loving others and making disciples.

A -

What do you need to *adjust* on each of the above?

D -

What <u>will</u> you *do* about it?

CHAPTER 9 - WHO WILL WALK ALONGSIDE YOU?

As we stated in the introduction, even though this is the greatest adventure you will ever be on, it is still not about you. It's about Jesus and the people he is calling to Himself through your new church. You are not alone, you are surrounded with a larger web of relationships, all of which will be affected in some way by the decisions you make as a spiritual leader. We don't exist in a vacuum. We are relational creatures who live in an interconnecting web of relationships, and you won't be starting this new church in a vacuum either. All kinds of people will be affected by your mission, those you will be leaving from, those who will be going with you, and those whom you will be going to. Let's look at some of these relationships and what you will need to be aware of in the process.

Your Parent Church

For planters who are being sent out – "birth out" – of a "parent church," there is a web of relationships that you already have. Each of these relationships comes with a set of expectations and responsibilities. Those people who are part of your sending church, the pastor, leaders and congregation all have them in differing aspects and varying degrees. Depending on the church's level of participation in sending you, in vision, people, and finances, there will be expectations in direct proportion. They have invested in you and to some extent are joining you on the journey. They want to see you succeed and prosper in your ministry. They have bought into you, your vision – or both! If they are Kingdom-minded, then their heart is to see God expand His reign and rule through the work of your plant. Understanding how to strengthen, cultivate and maintain these relationships can be significant in avoiding future conflict with your parent church.

Clarification is essential. The clarification of roles, future relationships and expectations regarding the sending church pastor and congregation should all be spelled out, and in some way put down on paper so that all parties involved can know what to expect. Communicating to all involved the agreed upon elements will serve to clear up misconceptions that could lead to future misunderstanding, and to relational difficulty.

For instance, what does the parent church pastor expect from you as the planter? What do you expect from him or her? What kind of input, accountability or direction will they be contributing – or expect to contribute? For the congregation – what can they expect from you, and what communication will they receive about your progress? Are they expecting you to be an extension of their church, with similar vision and values, similar ministries?

The congregation of your parent church is a vital resource for you, and you should do all you can to cultivate that relationship through vision casting for your new church and through good communication. Your sending congregation can aid you in your quest for the Kingdom in there specific pays: they can *pray*, *give* and *go*.

Pray: You can enlist intercessors to pray for you, your family and the life and ministry of your new church. As we always say, **prayer is the fuel the church runs on**, and you can never have too many people praying for you! Recruiting several dozen people to pray for you and the ministry on a daily basis will energize your ministry in a n essential. Creating a feedback and reporting loop through which you let them know of ministry success and prayer requests is key to maintaining your base of prayer. If someone is committed enough to pray for you, you can commit to regular updates. Email, a blog, a password-protected page on your website, a newsletter are all ways to close that communications loop.

Give: With the Senior Pastor of the parent church's permission, you can develop a donor base to provide initial funding or support for the new work. It may be as simple as a special offering being received, or as detailed as monthly support commitments being elicited. Whatever form it takes, this is resource that flows from the relationship with the parent church congregation. A compelling vision birthed of the Lord and well presented will have funding flow to it. When you paint the picture of God's preferred future for this church, remember to attach the price tag. People need to know what this adventure is going to cost, and you need to have a well developed first year budget that can be communicated and clearly explained. They will want to know the outcomes, the transformed lives and how you will accomplish them, but they will fund you at the prompting of the Lord.

Go: This one has three parts: **short term**, **long term** and **permanent**. Some people will want to come and support this new work with their presence, gifting and finances, but will want to do it only for three to six months. These short-timers can be a great blessing if you are doing any kind of large group gathering or Sunday worship service. Have these people "sign-up" by communicating their commitment level and length of service. Again, put the expectations in writing. The longer-term person might be with you for one to two years, but then want to return to the mothership. As with the short timer, validate the commitment level and get it down on paper. The person making a permanent transition to the new congregation should likewise have the details spelled out and confirmed. These are the people who will get more of your time and become the core community, which we will discuss next. All three of these groups, the short term, long term and permanent, need to communicate with the senior pastor of the parent church their intentions, seeking guidance and blessing. The senior pastor should have veto power over who goes. You should not receive anyone into the new work if the senior pastor does not agree to their participation. There is the issue of maintaining the health and viability of the parent church, as well as issues of the personal spiritual and emotional health of the person wishing to participate. Both of these could preclude someone from becoming involved. Joining you, while potentially helpful to you, may not be in the best interest of the parent church or the individual. Since this is about the Kingdom, and not about you, these concerns should always trump your personal needs and desires.

Core Community

The core community, whether it is sent with you from the parent church or is gathered through you by Jesus, is the defining component of this new church. The talents, gifts and spiritual empowerment from the Holy Spirit will release the mission of the church. In other words, who they are in Christ and in personality and what they can bring to the table determine much about the church. How they relate with you and each other, and you with them, will set the tone and environment for the new church.

We have discussed gathering and developing your core community in a previous chapter, but what do you expect of them, and they of you? What does it mean to be a member of this community? What is their role, their "rights" so to speak, in this covenant relationship, and what are their "responsibilities?" Detailing all this forms your ecclesiology, or understanding of what "church" is. Essentially a woven fabric of relationship, the warp and woof of your new church will only be as strong as those relationships are. 1 Peter 2:5 uses another analogy, that of a spiritual house, wherein people are "living stones" being shaped into a habitation of the Spirit. The mortar that holds the wall together is the loving relationships expressed amongst the stones. Enunciating the expectations of all involved will help maintain the "unity of the spirit in the bond of peace" (Ephesians 4:3 ESV).

Denominational Overseers

The people definitely have expectations, and what they expect can and will shape the implementation of your church planting project. Depending on your polity, these expectations, can be significant and specific, or minimal and general in scope. Any resourcing in the form of training or finances is usually tied to fulfilling these expectations – and appropriately so. Those denominations or networks that are investing in church planting have a stewardship responsibility, both spiritually and financially, and true stewardship can only be engaged and realized through standards to which someone can be held accountable. They must know that the church plant they are sponsoring and facilitating will be of the same spiritual DNA as their movement, and that any funding expended will be done so in the most effective manner. Understanding this from the outset will put you as the planter in the right frame of mind to relate properly with those overseeing your ministry. Remember, one of the issues we have already discussed is the test of submission, and you will re-live that test at various times and in various ways. At each occurrence, you must pass that test to progress in your walk with Jesus and your ministry.

There is usually some kind of reporting expected from denominational or network overseers, as well as specific steps in a process that is required for the planter to pass through in the journey. There may be regular gatherings or conferences you are expected to attend. Do all that is asked of you. All this is appropriate. Your job is to learn what the expectations in all these areas are, and gain an understanding of how you can fulfill them. These officials are leaders are gatekeepers in your movement, and while they can be a source of frustration, they are also a channel of the Lord's blessing and provision. Managing and maintaining these relationships is a high priority for you.

A note concerning reporting to any denominational leaders who may have been forced to read this book: what you are measuring in relation to the progress of your church plants is probably the wrong thing. In post-Christian America, an organic approach to church planting that we are suggesting in this book will differ significantly from other church planting projects. First, the church may take longer to develop, but the maturity of disciples and their commitment to Christ will be deeper. The slower growth rate is due primarily to the fact that we are suggesting evangelistic church planting, as opposed to transfer growth church planting. You may have a crowd, but you may not have disciples of Jesus. Give grace on timelines, and do not despise the mustard seed in the day of its small beginnings (Matthew 13:31-32, Zechariah 4:6-10). We normally count the ABC's: attendance, buildings and cash. In this day of salvation as a journey and a process, rather than counting "decisions," perhaps a better means of evaluation is the significant conversations being had with those outside the faith, the number of those truly becoming disciples, and how many true leaders are in development. We advocate that you not count anything, rather go experience the core community and see what quality and quantity of the life of Jesus is like in the people being reached through the church. But if you do have to count something, consider what we suggested as a means of evaluating fruitfulness.

Mentors

Mentors are those people in our life that God has used to space us and crafts us. Many times, these relationships are life-long. Reaffirming and renegotiating your relationship with your mentors as you enter into a church planting process is wise. They can be strong sources of encouragement and support in the midst of the battle. Those who have ministry background can offer advice from their experience on pastoral and ministry issues, and add wisdom to your zeal.

Seven months into his first church plant, Tom hit the wall and had enough. Living in a rural setting, planting in a small town, a core of people had been reached for Christ and gathered into a small group. Some of the personalities were interesting to say the least. It was February, and in New Hampshire where he and his wife Cathy were planting, this means temperatures below zero and lots of snow. Lots of snow. In fact, on the particular night this story takes place, there was a blizzard raging in full force outside the cabin they had rented for a home. Tom never knew that twenty people could have so many problems – and cause an equal amount in relationship with each other and create so much stress. In Tom's mind the people were great, but this group definitely put the "fun" in "dysfunctional."

So we come to the fateful night, which was indeed dark and stormy. At issue was the fact that Tom and Cathy needed help in the form of input and counsel on how to help minister to these people. Despite all the promises of relational support from the mother church forty-five miles away, there was only one person who had maintained a supportive relationship with them, namely Tom's mentor Leo. Tom, having reached his limit, and in the midst of "intense fellowship" (read: argument) with his wife, declared he was going to quit this church planting thing, give up on ministry and pursue his career again. Cathy told him through her tears, "If you are really going to quit, pick up the phone and call Leo and tell him you quit right now." Of course, right now was Three A.M. So Tom did. He dialed Leo's number, and upon hearing his mentor's sleepy voice on the other end of the line, he said "Leo, this is Tom. I QUIT!" and slammed down the phone. He put on his parka and pack boots and went out into the snow and minus twenty-two degree night. About fifteen feet from the door, he slipped on the ice, fell and smacked his head. After lying there for several minutes, crying and crying out to God, he crawled back to the house, covered with snow, wet and cold. Re-entering the house, he found Cathy on the phone with the ever-faithful Leo, who had called back. Through her sobs she indicated Leo wanted to talk with Tom. Getting on the phone, Leo said to Tom, "So, are we having a little problem out there?" Tom proceeded to download his frustration about the people, his lack of ability to address the issues, and the absence of support. After about five minutes of listening, Leo interrupted and said, "Listen, take two aspirin and call me in the morning. Go to bed. We can talk more tomorrow. It'll be alright." And that's how Leo saved Tom's ministry – and it would not be the last time. In fact, to the date of this writing, Leo and his wife Mollie continue to be a source of great encouragement and support to Tom and Cathy.

The moral of the story is this: before you plant, check in with your mentors, invite them into the mix, and get the number to the phone they will answer at Three A.M.

Coaches

Having a church planting coach walk alongside you in this process is essential. As it is often said, mentors **pour in**, but coaches **draw out** what God has already placed there. Coaching very often will focus on the sodalic, or "task" aspect of planting, helping you think through the process. They help the planter maintain focus in the midst of a sea of distraction. Staying on task can be difficult for a planter, because of the demands of life, ministry and working a job if the planter is bi-vocational. The work that goes into a church plant, the difficulty of building something from nothing, combined with spiritual resistance, life issues and the pastoral needs of a growing flow can pull the planter in a number of directions at once. It is common for planters to get off beam within two or three weeks of living life and doing ministry. This makes regular monthly coaching sessions imperative, to keep the planter on course and moving forward.

Coaches can help planters think through various aspects of starting the new church, probing and challenging with questions, very much like the Rabbis of old, making the hearer think, learn and grow. But not anyone will do for a coach. Someone who has some background in ministry, and more specifically in church planting, can be of great assistance. Ideally, a church planter who has been trained and developed as a church planting coach would be the best choice. The coach training provides this person the skills in helping lead someone in a journey of self-discovery, not so much in "telling" the planter what to do, but in "asking" questions that lead to understanding. Having that trained person be an seasoned church planter lends an experiential component, allowing the coaching to operate more fully inside the planters frame of reference.

Here again it is important to determine the expectations of both the coach and the planter in writing. As a guide on your quest, your coach needs to know what you are looking for and relate to you how he/she feels he/she can best serve you.

All these relationships we have discussed form the backdrop of your planting endeavor. Remember, you are not on this quest for yourself, but for the purposes of Jesus and His Kingdom, and you are not on the journey alone.

Chapter Nine R.E.A.D. Questions - "Who Will Walk Alongside You?"

R -

- Based on your *reflection*, list the three major things that the Holy Spirit spoke to your heart regarding the expectations of various relationships.
- *Reflect* on how you will relate to various groups or persons discussed in the chapter.

E -

- Based on the new awareness that you have gained, how would you *evaluate* your current life and church plant in
- *Evaluate* your current process for validating roles and determining expectations?

A -

What do you need to *adjust* on each of the above?

D -

What <u>will</u> you *do* about it?

CHAPTER 10 - HOW WILL YOU COMPLETE YOUR TRAINING?

In the epic *Star Wars* saga, in Episode V - *The Empire Strikes Back*, young Luke Skywalker has been under the instruction of the 800 year-old Jedi Master, Yoda. Having a premonition of the future of his friends suffering in agony, Luke abandons his path of learning, rushing off to confront Darth Vader. Yoda cries out "Remember your training! Save you, it can!" Before you rush off on your own adventure, make sure you can complete your training, planning and preparing for this new work as much as possible.

Tom was once assigned to train a church planter in his local church by his denomination. This church planting couple came from a denominational Bible college, and needed some seasoning before they could be released to plant. Full of their vision of the future, they were offended by the denomination's requirement that they serve in Tom's church for a season. They felt they were prepared, and said "We want to be out of here in six months. Just tell us what we need to do to plant the church." Not exactly a teachable attitude. For almost two years this couple and their family failed to truly take advantage of the training resourcing offered them. Finally, they pressed to be allowed to attend a church planters training intensive. On the second day of the intensive, they realized how much they didn't know, and how much Tom had been trying to teach them. They apologized to Tom for their attitude, but the time had already been wasted. The couple eventually did attempt a church plant. After struggling along at thirty to forty people in attendance for several years, the plant ultimate closed when the planters burned out. Sadly, today that couple is divorced.

It is also sad to say that this story is not all that uncommon. What is the lesson to be learned? As complete a preparation as possible is essential before launching out in your church planting quest. We know none of us are ever truly "ready" for what the Lord calls us to do in partnership with Him, but being teachable and accessing all the learning opportunities possible is essential.

The Apostle Paul, educated, and a "Pharisee of Pharisees" went through an intense period of preparation prior to beginning the fullness of his apostolic ministry and endeavoring in his true calling. He participated in ministry, preached and taught and evangelized, connected with Peter and James after three years, but it was fourteen years after his Damascus Road experience that he was released to function fully in his apostolic calling (Galatians 1-2). Release, when it comes appropriately and not by our will, comes when we are ready as persons to face the challenge of planting. Some take more preparation, some less. Planting itself is designed to be a growth opportunity for us in character, in faith and in ministry competency. Such release often comes in proportion to our development: once you are proven faithful in little you can be trusted to be faithful in much. You must do all that you can do to prepare for the task ahead.

What You Can Do to Prepare

There are many things which you can do to prepare, and in the words of Luke Skywalker, "complete what you have begun." Here are a few things that will help you on your Kingdom quest:

- **Read on the subject voraciously.** It seems that you are already doing this, since you have gotten this far in this book! But don't stop there. There is a growing body of literature on church planting, and like all things, you will need discernment on what you read.

Remember this, Christianity in the West is almost always approached from a pragmatic standpoint. "If it works, do it" is the motto. This is an outcome driven approach, with the measure being weekend service attendance. Don't go there. Instead look for principle-based, non-model specific resources that focus on making disciples through a relational process. Having 1,000 people in a service is awesome, but it is not your goal. It is having those 1,000 (or 25 or 150 or 300) be true disciples of Jesus Christ. As our friend, Ralph Moore likes to say, "Hey, cheer up! If you have more than 120 disciples, then your doing better than Jesus (Acts 1:15)!"

- **Have a church planting assessment done.** If you are called to be a church planter, run to it. If not, run from it. Please, please, please, if you are not called to church plant, then don't try it at home. Find some other means of ministry expression. There are many groups that offer a behavioral assessment for church planters, and can generate an assessment report from an interview process. If you haven't already done so, and before you take a step further on your quest, stop right now and get a church planting assessment done. It will show you your strengths on which the Lord wants to build ministry, as well as your growth areas that need further development. Many times those who discover through this process that they are not called to plant find that the assessment report is a great tool for determining what kind of ministry would be the best fit for them, leading to satisfying and rewarding contribution to the Kingdom.
- **Work through a church planting resource.** Find a resource tool that walks you through the development and implementation of your church planting process. There are many workbooks and "toolkits" out there. One we collaborated on is called *Beyond*

Church Planting and is available from our publisher, ChurchSmart Resources. These kinds of stand-alone, self-guided tools are great at making a first pass at developing a plan for your plant. Put some effort into it, and you will be surprised what you discover together with the Lord.

- **Attend a church planting intensive.** In our ministry at Praxis (www.praxiscenter.org) we have a church planters training intensive which is, oddly enough, called The Quest. It walks you through an in-depth development of a pathway for starting your new church. There are several other good training intensives out there, but the same discernment rules apply as indicated with books.
- **Talk to church planters, both those who have succeeded, and those who have not.** Connecting with successful planters builds your faith, connecting with those who have not succeeded builds your wisdom. Talk with both kinds, if you can find them. Don't become enamored with what the successful ones are doing: Learn from them, but build your own wineskin. Don't adopt their model. Find what the Father is doing in your city or town, and do it with Him (John 5:19). Likewise, when interviewing the unsuccessful planter, expect to hear pain and difficulty. Don't let fear take your heart, but learn from any mistakes you can glean.
- **Finally – and first of all – pray like crazy.** We place this last in the list not out of any sort of ranking, but for emphasis. Prayer prepares and trains the soul – your heart and mind – and brings transformation. And that's what you have to give away – a changed life. You can't give away what you don't have. Your plan might be awesome, your music hot, your structure the coolest there is. Your church could be the "latest in church technology," but without living a life that is constantly being transformed, your package will be

slick, but your content will be slim. Pray and build your relationship with the Lord, learning to hear His voice. Pray and get your marching orders from Him daily (Mark 1:35). Pray for laborers for your harvesting team (Luke 10:2). Pray in the midst of trial like Jesus, and be found justified by God (Luke 4). Pray for empowerment like the Apostles, praying for ten days, and see the fire fall on your core community (Acts 2). Pray like Daniel for breakthrough, praying for twemty-one days (Daniel 10:2). Whatever you do in preparation for your Kingdom quest, pray. Then pray some more!

May the Lord bless you as you seek first His kingdom and His righteousness, having no thought for yourself or your own needs. May he make your quest for His Kingdom indeed fruitful.

Chapter Ten R.E.A.D. Questions -
"How will you complete your training?"

R -

- Based on your *reflection*, list the three major things that the Holy Spirit spoke to your heart regarding completing your training.

E -

- Based on the new awareness that you have gained, how would you *evaluate* preparation for church planting?

A -

What do you need to *adjust* on each of the above?

D -

What <u>will</u> you *do* about it?

APPENDIX – DETERMINING YOUR PERSONAL VALUES

Knowing who you are in Christ is an essential part of your preparation for planting. Values define who you are and how you personally will engage in the thing called ministry. We have included this section for you to work through as a means of self discovery. Remember, the focus of this appendix is about you, not the church you desire to plant. Approach it from that framework. **Think both being and doing – not just ministry.** Think holistically, about life, family, relationships, etc. What is important to you about these things? Know this: some of your church's values will differ from your personal values. That's OK, but knowing your values will influence the overall process of developing your congregational values. So, jump in and get started!

Key Elements of Story

1. Knowing our stories helps us know ourselves. Therefore, as you write your story you will want to list the key circumstances and events of your life.

2. Recognizing the driving forces and influences in your life. Who and what experiences have influenced your life?

3. Discovering the key God-moments in your life.

4. As your write your story, what surfaces as key moments of change and transformation in your life?

5. What were the critical moments of your life? The crisis stages? What did you learn from these situations?

6. From your timeline list, from birth to present, that which depicts the following:

    - Significant events and circumstances (e.g. conflict with family, taking a church, etc)
    - The people who most influenced your life
    - The key God-moments in your life (e.g. your salvation, calling, etc.)

7. From your timeline and your story, now take the critical moments and people of your life and list them below.

INFLUENTIAL MOMENT
VALUE LEARNED/CONVICTION
1.
2.
3.
4.
5.
6.
7.
8.
9.
10.

8. What key moments or people have most shaped your life?

WRITING YOUR STORY

The Driver: Your Values

> "A man without a purpose is like a ship without a rudder—a waif, a nothing, a no man." Thomas Carlyle

Values: Things We Live By

What then are values?

Simply stated, it is "Why" we do what we do because of what we want (Vision). Defines intent.

1. Values are constant – they rarely change – may expand or become more focused.

2. Values are passionate – they generate emotion and energy.

3. Values are based on a Biblical worldview that submits to the authority of the Lordship of Jesus.

4. Values are our core convictions – they influence everything we do. We see by the chart that values have great influence on our attitudes, which then affect our behavior, which in turn validates our value system. Thus what you really want in life or out of life is what will actually effect your behavior.

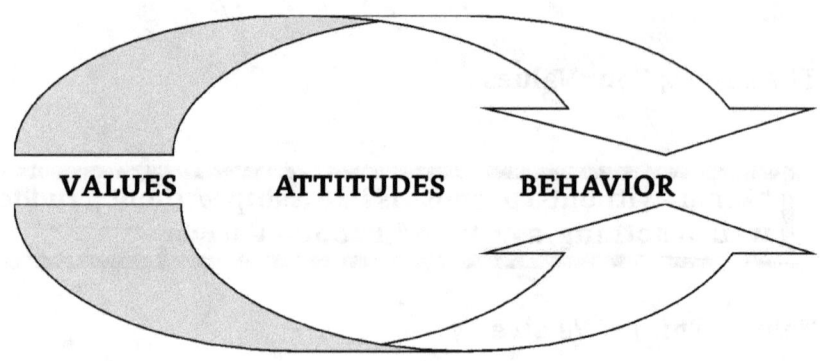

VALUES   ATTITUDES   BEHAVIOR

5. Values drive our ministry. It is the **why** that underlies vision and mission. In essence, values communicate what is important. It is the filter by which all behavior and energy will be evaluated. In this sense, we can say that values are constant, passionate and biblical.

What Values Are Not

1. Values are not necessarily our statement of faith, belief, purpose, or theology. What is often believed is not what is valued. For example, the demons believe in God (James 2:19), but they do not value the Lordship of Jesus to the point of submission. You may believe in evangelism, but do you do it? If you do, it is a value.

2. Values do not involve the methods nor programs we employ. The methods and programs are the delivery systems of our values. As you can see, values have great influence on our attitudes, which then affects our behavior. Jesus said it this way,

> "For where your treasure is, there your heart will be also." (Matt. 6:21) *It becomes apparent that if what we want is in conflict with what we believe, then*

> what we want will win. All the promises in the world will not change a thing unless we accept responsibility for our behavior in terms of what we want. What you value is then where your treasure is.

Some Examples

When it comes to a church, Lyle Schaller writes, *"The most important single element of any corporate, congregational, or denominational culture, however, is the value system."* (Getting Things Done, p. 152) Based on Acts 2:42-47, we see that the Jerusalem church valued the following:

1. They valued teaching (2:42-43).
2. They valued relationship (2:42).
3. They valued prayer (2:42).
4. They valued community (2:44-46).
5. They valued praise and worship (2:47).
6. They valued evangelism (2:47).

Jerusalem Church Values	Jerusalem Church Behavior
Teaching	Devoted themselves to the apostle's teaching
Relationship	Met together in homes
Prayer	Small group prayer
Community	Shared things in common with generosity
Praise and Worship	Sang in the homes
Evangelism	People were getting saved because of hearing the gospel.

If we turn to Acts 6:1-7, we see a values driven decision performed by the leaders of the early church. There was a potential church split between the Grecian Jews and the Hebraic Jews. The Grecian Jews felt the Hebraic Jews were neglecting their widows in the daily disbursement of food. The Twelve called a meeting. Instead of taking valuable time to involve themselves in the matter, they made a decision based on a value that they had to give themselves to prayer and teaching of the word. As a result, they decided to appoint seven highly qualified people to take care of the matter. **Values influence behavior**. What we value is demonstrated most clearly in what we do.

Writing Out Your Values

Herein you will write out seven to ten core values that you hold. It will be apparent from your life story what these might be. These are things you would die for. All values, on paper, sound wonderful. However, the test of a value that is true to life is simple. A **"real"** value is one that is lived out.

Values are something that everyone possesses. Vocing a value does not necessarily mean that it drives our life. For example, there are three different ways to define values. The first level of values is **"aspirations"**. This is when a person admires and even thinks favorably of something. However, the value does not impact his life. The second level is what is called **"preferred"** values. A person who has **"preferred"** values is someone who definitely believes. There is conviction that resounds. Scripture explains this for us: "You believe there is one God. Good! Even the demons believe that -- and shudder." (Jm. 2:19, NIV) There is no doubt that the belief is strong but the heart is not submitted to it. As a result, there is very little or no impact to a life. The last level is **"real"** values. These are values that are embraced with conviction and a submitted heart. The life is impacted and the value is lived out. Maybe that is the best description of a value -- something that is lived out.

Key Questions To Help Determine Your Values

1. Is what you believe what you value? If so, how would you know?

> **ASSESSMENT CRITERION (T.E.R.M.):** Time, Energy, Reflection and Money: If you value something, your time, energy, reflection and money will be given to it. Take a few minutes and review the past thirty days of your life and

> look at where your time, importance, money and energy have gone. For example, if you say you value family, how much time, importance money and energy have you spent with your family each week?

2. What do you believe are the most important aspects of the Christian faith?

3. When people talk about you, what would you want them to be saying about you?

Action Step

1. Make a list of what you believe are the non-negotiables of your life – those convictions and behaviors by which your life is governed.

    Values Exercise

2. From the above, now take your values and narrow them down to seven to ten core values.

3. After you have written out your seven to ten core values, apply the assessment tool of **"Time, Energy, Reflection and Money"** to it. From the assessment make a note describing what kind of value it is. For example:

| VALUE | CATEGORY |

"My wife and family are my most significant ministry." Preferred

"I value dignity and will always treat people honorably."   Real

VALUE	CATEGORY
1.	
2.	
3.	
4.	
5.	
6.	
7.	
8.	
9.	
10.	

www.ingramcontent.com/pod-product-compliance
Lightning Source LLC
LaVergne TN
LVHW051522070426
835507LV00023B/3255